Horse-Drawn Vehicles in Colour

By the same author

Fire Engines in Colour
Lorries, Trucks and Vans 1927–1973

HORSE-DRAWN VEHICLES
SINCE 1760
in Colour

by
ARTHUR INGRAM

Colour Plates
by
David Dowland and Joyce Smith

BLANDFORD PRESS
Poole Dorset

First published in 1977

Link House, West Street, Poole, Dorset. BH15 1LL.

ISBN 0 7137 0820 4

Set in 11/12 pt Imprint by Woolaston Parker Ltd.
Printed in Great Britain by Richard Clay (The Chaucer Press) Ltd.
Colour illustrations printed by Sackville Press
(Billericay) Ltd.

CONTENTS

PREFACE

This book of horse-drawn vehicles brings together for the first time a selection of both passenger and goods carrying vehicles which are shown in full colour and adequately described. Most other publications on the subject have been concerned with the better known private vehicles and much has been written on the more glamorous mail coaches. Here we try to redress the balance by showing some of the more humble carts, wagons and vans which literally rubbed shoulders with the fine coaches and carriages of the period. No attempt has been made to produce a history of all the various kinds of vehicles that have been produced; that indeed would need several volumes of this size. Neither do we give the farm vehicle more than a cursory glance as this is a subject on its own and will later form the subject of another book in this series.

Following the descriptions of the colour plates will be found reference to the materials used in the building of the vehicles mentioned and the various skilled men required to put them together. For the uninitiated diagrams are provided to explain some of the words used to describe the various parts of the vehicles and the glossary of vehicle type terms is provided in the hope that it will assist in easier understanding, although because of a lack of accepted vehicle nomenclature the reader may well be no further out of the wood!

Although this volume is not as large as one might have wished it is nevertheless hoped that the reader might find himself getting a measure of satisfaction approaching that gained in producing it. Research has proved particularly rewarding and grateful thanks go to *Old Motor Magazine* for access to their considerable collection, to Mr E. Paget-Thomson of Hull Transport Museum and to Mr Milligan at the North Western Museum of Science and Industry.

London
1977

Arthur Ingram

CONSTRUCTION OF VEHICLES

The horse-drawn vehicle as a whole was divisible into two main parts, 1) the carriage or gear, and 2) the body. The first part consisted of the wheels, axles, springs, forecarriage parts, fifth wheel, perch, futchells and splinter bar or as a whole the running gear which carried the bodywork. The body was the upper part which contained the load or carried the passengers, and the driver. In early designs the driver's seat was often carried on the carriage but in later designs his seat was attached to the body proper so that he had the benefit of any springing fitted, or if of springless design his seat was itself carried on small springs.

The body came in an infinite variety of designs and the various parts used were according to its style. It may have been of the most simple flat platform for carrying goods or it may have been a most intricate and ornate coach for carrying important personages. It could be constructed almost entirely of timber and iron as in the former design or it may have needed all kinds of materials including silk, leather, horsehair, glass, brass, silver, bone and mother of pearl, as in the latter vehicle. Most vehicles came somewhere between the two extremes with the goods carrying types being constructed mainly of timber, iron, leather and canvas with the passengers carrying designs using more leather, horsehair, silk, rubber, brass and glass for comfort and finish.

Because of the diverse materials used in vehicle construction it was only natural that many and various skills were required in its completion. Because the most difficult part of coachbuilding was the construction of the wheels, the wheelwright came to be known as the builder of vehicles. As the vehicles became more complicated in their design and a higher degree of finish was demanded so the need for specialist craftsmen was generated. The development of specialization led to the employment of a designer or draughtsman to produce a design and accurate drawings firstly to show the customer what he was getting and latterly as a guide to the actual builders.

In the days of local wheelwrights building simple farm vehicles a lot of information was stored in their heads, and much of the construction carried out by experience from previous vehicles. Often their eye would tell them if a certain dimension or detail was right and the variety of different styles built was limited. Later the cant board was used to store details of vehicle measurements and this was more durable than a sheet of drawing paper, but of little use in explaining a design to a customer.

Having decided on a particular design the next step was to get the various craftsmen to produce their particular part for the complete vehicle. The carriage makers produced the carriage or gear, the wheelwrights the wheels and the bodymaker the body. For the ironwork a blacksmith would be called upon, although in greater degrees of specialization the ironwork may have been further divided between an axle tree maker, a spring maker and a general smith for the other ironwork.

If the vehicle was to be nicely finished it was possible that a woodcarver was required and then it was placed in the hands of the coach trimmers for lining and upholstery and this section was further divided to include lacemakers, ivory workers, embroiderers for the interior fittings and curriers for the leather parts. The painters now had to spend time on the vehicle preparing the surface, putting on coats of paint, rubbing it down, filling the imperfections, putting on finishing coats, varnishing and polishing. Special artists or heraldic painters may also have been required for their particular skills and then lamp makers were needed for the lamps and glaziers for the glass. A locksmith might be necessary for the door locks and fittings and a gilder was called upon should the coach body require the application of gold leaf.

According to the size and extent of the coachbuilder most of the work was done at his own establishment, or much of the finishing was passed to other specialist firms or individual craftsmen. Not that the list of tradesmen mentioned above is complete. There were others that may have been called upon such as trunkmakers, blind makers, harness makers, floorcloth and carpet layers, platers, ivory workers, chasers and turners, all lending their particular skill to fulfil a special need.

Regarding the materials used it will be gathered from the foregoing that wood and iron or steel formed the major part of the horse-drawn vehicle. Wood was used for the major parts of the carriage and body with metal being used for strength either in its own right or as a strengthening to the wood parts requiring it.

In early vehicles wood was used in great bulk to produce the strength required for carrying a heavy load over indifferent surfaces. With improvements in roads and springing there was a gradual lightening of some vehicles which rendered large section timbers unnecessary. With the increased use of iron strapping or plating it was possible to reduce the size of some parts and a further form of lightening was possible by means of bevelling, carving and generally shaping parts. This form of lightening was only possible where the strength of the part would not be materially reduced beyond a safe limit and it often helped the look of the vehicle by removing some of the harsh square lines.

The types of timber used included ash, oak, elm, beech, mahogany, cedar, deal, pine, lancewood, birch, hickory and quite a lot of others in various parts of the world. Naturally the early wheelwrights had to use whatever timber was available. Often a compromise had to be reached between availability, suitability and price.

Generally speaking ash was preferred for framing, wheel felloes, axle beds, bolsters, shafts and cart sides. Oak was for wheel spokes, body framing, bolsters and sides; elm was favourite for wheel naves, floorboards and planks, and beech for axle beds and bolsters.

Mahogany was liked for body panelling, cedar being used if the panel was to be covered because it did not take paint so well. Deal was a cheaper form of flooring than elm and pine boards were suitable for roof panels. Lancewood was at one time preferred for shafts until the fashion for curved shafts precluded its use. Ash was also liked for shafts because of its great strength and possibility of bending. Birch was used for thin panels which could be bent and possibly covered.

The above analysis is neither complete nor mandatory as a glance through a few old specifications will reveal. Glancing at a design for a greengrocer's cart of 1901 we find that oak is specified for the body framing while the next specification which is for a removal van lists the frame as being of oak and panelling in mahogany, although a note is appended saying that if this was not available then pine or American ash may be substituted. An 1899 design for a forage cart lists the shafts as being of 'tough ash, hickory or American elm' and the panelling of 'American birch or soft pine' while the body framing should be of 'best English oak'. So it becomes apparent that there is no hard and fast rule for the timber used; there are definite preferences but it all depends on the location, availability and cost.

Iron was the principal metal used in vehicle construction and this was originally forged into the required shape by the smith using his own fire and hammer. The introduction of steel springs brought in a more specialized material and often the springmaker was himself a specialist making springs for a number of coachbuilders. The major metal parts on a vehicle were often considerable in total, with a high proportion of the undercarriage being made from iron on some carriages. A lot of this ironwork is apparent when looking at say a landau or barouche, while there is still more used for strengthening the body although it is not noticeable. With the delicate, slender curved body on a canoe landau (Plate 26) the body framing was 'well ironed', according to the term used, or it would not have been long before it showed signs of sagging and the doors would not function.

Other metals such as brass, gunmetal, copper, silver, lead and tin were used in lesser amounts for such things as rails, bearings, beading, door handles, body filling and lamps. Hides were used for fixed and folding heads, seats and upholstery and in closed carriages wool, silk and cotton materials would be used for cushions, lining and decoration. Horsehair was invariably used for cushion filling, glass for windows and rubber for tyres. Other small items might be made from flax, straw, ivory, whalebone, hemp and of course various glues and paints were needed for finishing the vehicle.

For an indication of the actual structure of a vehicle reference should be made to the line drawings preceding the glossary of terms at the end of this book. This is the kind of drawing prepared by the designer or draughtsman after a preliminary drawing showing the general layout of the vehicle had been tendered to the customer and approved by him.

In order to show sufficient detail of the method of framing

and jointing the body a working drawing would be produced to a scale of somewhere in the region of $\frac{3}{4}$ in. or $1\frac{1}{2}$ in. to one foot. Drawings to such scales were usually sufficient to show all the details required to enable construction to proceed. Should certain parts of the vehicle be so complicated as to render these drawings insufficient then detail drawings to a larger scale even up to full size would be produced. This would only be necessary with intricate fittings, elaborate carving or fine panel painting and lettering.

The line drawings are also included for the benefit of model makers and others who may be interested to see the method of construction of such vehicles. Unfortunately our page size prohibits the provision of drawings to a larger scale and the attention of the serious model vehicle builder is directed to the Science Museum in South Kensington who produce large scale drawings of a farm wagon and to specialists whose advertisements appear in the *Draught Horse* magazine. Some of the old journals contain many fine drawings of a variety of vehicles and titles of these will be found together with other useful publications in the bibliography at the end of the book.

In recent years there has been a tremendous revival of interest in old vehicles of all kinds and this has extended into the allied fields of machinery and equipment. However, in spite of the proliferation of the collecting, preservation and display cult, there are some for whom the true interest has always been in horses and they have never forsaken their affection and support whether it be for working horses, or just riding, driving or showing them.

So far as the working vehicles are concerned things did go to a very low ebb in the 1950's when, except for a handful of stalwarts, the working turnout virtually disappeared from the scene be it on farm land or road. As mentioned elsewhere it was in the hands of a few people that the concern for the working horse lay. Support was made up from brewers, farmers, general dealers, gypsies, seaside carriagemen, dairymen, costermongers, bakers and laundries. Even so over the years the working horse support group has been in steady decline and the carts, vans, drays, wagons, cabs, buses and carriages could be found rotting in hedgerows, rusting in odd corners and burning in scrapdealers' yards. In some areas the change was very gradual and extended over many years; dairies sometimes running horse-drawn, electric and petrol vehicles side by side for 30 years while others quickly ousted the horses from their employ. In some spheres of public transport the horse was replaced very early with cabs and buses going mechanical in the first and second decades of the century; a similar state of affairs prevailed with the personal transport of those who could afford it particularly as they could get someone to do the driving for them.

In the goods carrying sphere the change has taken much longer but the present day enthusiast seeking examples of trade vehicles will now only find them in a few isolated places. The old established collections of horse-drawn vehicles include very few commercial vehicles, consisting mainly of coaches and carriages which have remained in barns, coachhouses and private collections over the years. A few old bakers' vans and milk floats have found their uses either in the hands of general dealers or paraffin salesmen and occasionally an old van is to be found doubling as a hen house on a farm.

It is pleasantly reassuring when an old horse 'bus body is found on an allotment or sports field, and only as recently as 1976 the discovery and subsequent acquisition by London Transport of an 1881 horse tram caused great excitement. It is because of their original fine workmanship and materials that these old bodies survive. Often the body and undercarriage were parted early on by the new owners, the wheels and axles being useful to make a farm trailer and the body for adapting as a toolshed, henhouse or what have you. Luckily for the restorers and preservationists these old vehicles were often covered with roofing felt or corrugated iron and after this was stripped off a reasonably sound body might be found beneath. Failing this there is sometimes enough of the woodwork to form a basis of patterns for the substitution of new timbers, and I know of at least one vehicle restorer who makes his own replacement wheels! Luckily for those engaged in restoration work the job of fashioning old parts is not quite so difficult as with some other vehicles. At least the horse power can be procured even if it is not the genuine age, but imagine the difficulty of casting a replacement motor vehicle engine!

With each succeeding year the number and quality of vehicles that can be seen in museums, collections and shows steadily accelerates. Some of these retain much of their original construction, materials and finish while others have been considerably restored to a very high standard. To the purist some of the restoration and rebuilding leaves a lot to be desired, but at least it proves that there is a lot of enthusiasm about, and some vehicles are still with us which might not have been otherwise. To those intent on preserving these vehicles of the past generations, the first priority is to save them from destruction or further rotting by putting them in a safe place. Unfortunately there is not always a plentiful supply of good accommodation and it is a depressing sight to see attractive vehicles stored in places open to the four winds. Although this has a drying effect the vehicle is best put up on blocks to prevent further damage to the vulnerable wheels.

As well as in the various museums around the country which have collections or merely a couple of vehicles it is also heartening to see the occasional vehicle kept by other bodies. There are a number of hotels which have the odd stage coach, hotel 'bus or brougham outside to attract attention although it is a pity they are not better cared for.

1 Irish Outside Car Design peculiar to Ireland and used both as private vehicle and as vehicle for hire. Larger four wheel design used as road coaches.

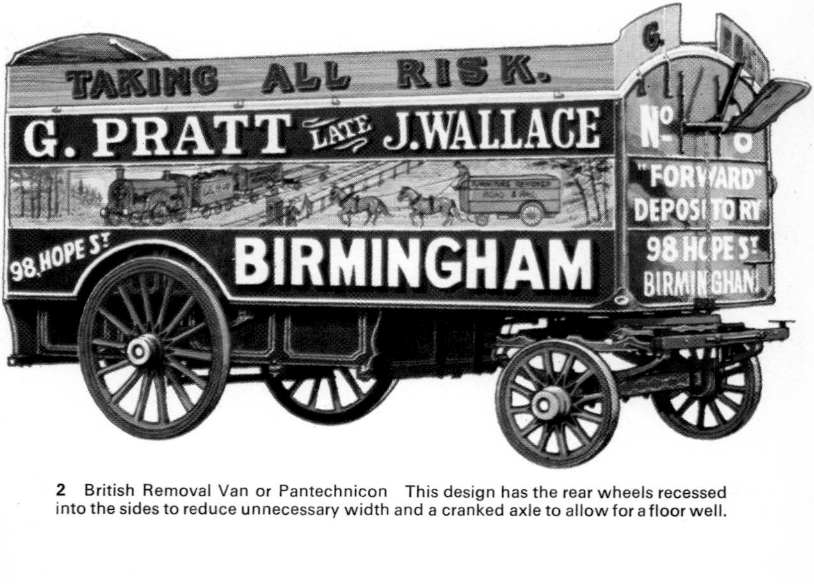

2 British Removal Van or Pantechnicon This design has the rear wheels recessed into the sides to reduce unnecessary width and a cranked axle to allow for a floor well.

3 British Gold State Coach Revealing all the lavishness that can be bestowed on a Royal Coach this specimen can be seen in the Royal Mews of Buckingham Palace.

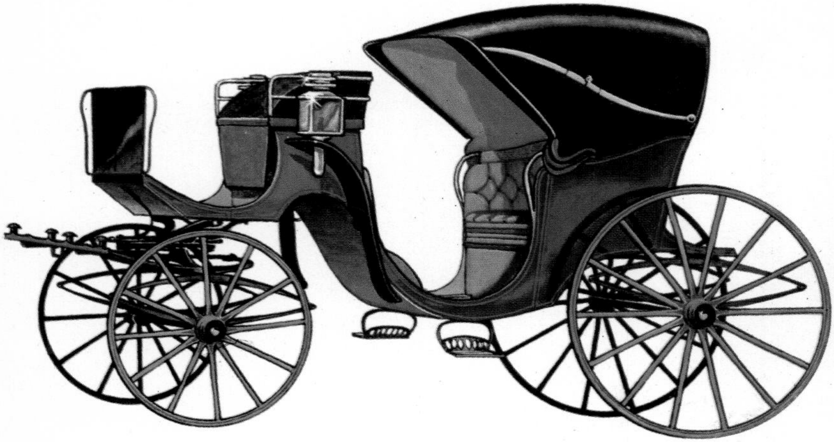

4 American Cabriolet A late nineteenth century north American design in its original European style.

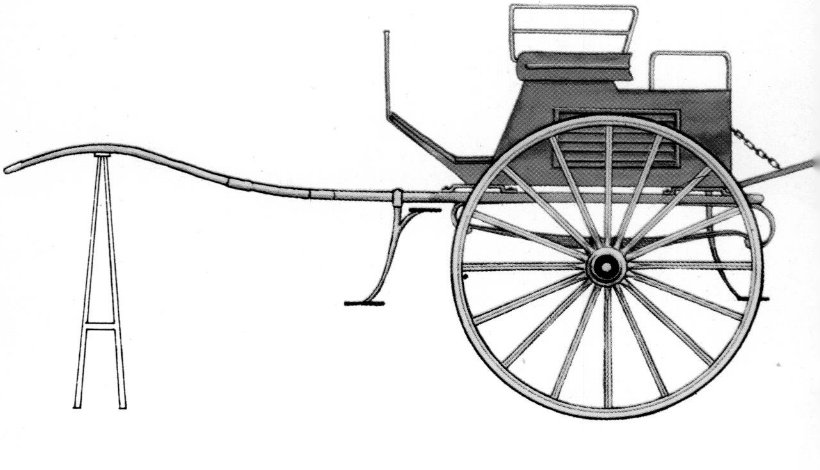

5 British Dog Cart Basic design of dog cart used for transporting hunting dogs.

6 Australian Bow Wagon Name derived from 'bows' over wheels which were to prevent load of harvested crops from fouling wheels.

7 American Farmer's Wagon Most simple form of wagon used by farmers, settlers and homesteaders.

8 British Governess Cart Light and safe transport for the children of the household and their governess or nanny.

9 American Prairie Schooner Style of vehicle used by settlers on long journeys across vast new areas of the north American continent when land was offered very cheaply to whoever cared to work it.

10 Australian Oil and Colourman's Wagon Plain design of low sided wagon for general goods.

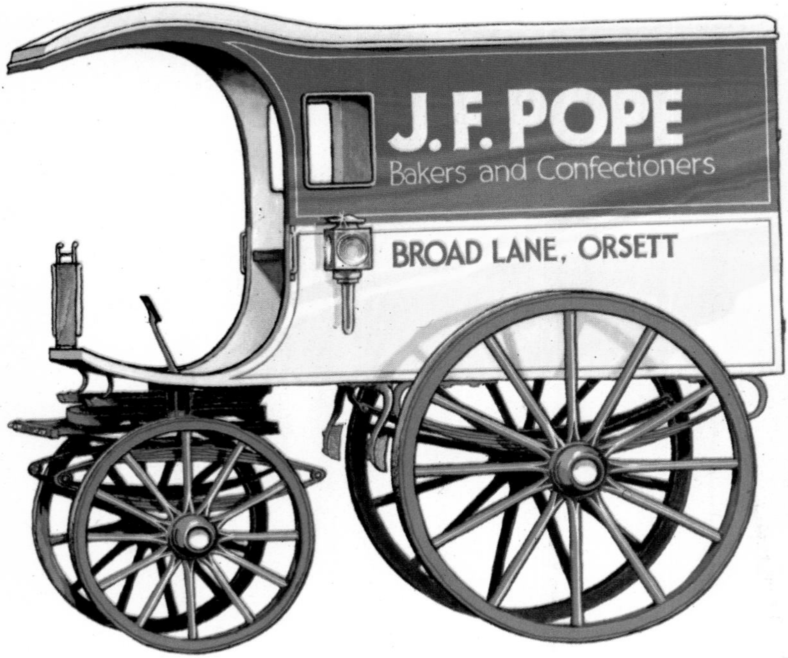

11 British Camel Top Van A popular style of trades van.

12 North American Logging Truck Heavy style of double truck for moving giant redwood logs.

13 American Gooseneck Truck Simple but practical low height freight truck useful for carrying heavy or tall loads.

14 British Wagonette Brake Popular style of passenger vehicle for touring and day trips. Space between seats used for picnic hampers and umbrellas! Note precarious perch for conductor or guard.

15 American Emergency Wagon An invaluable vehicle for trolley and streetcar operators.

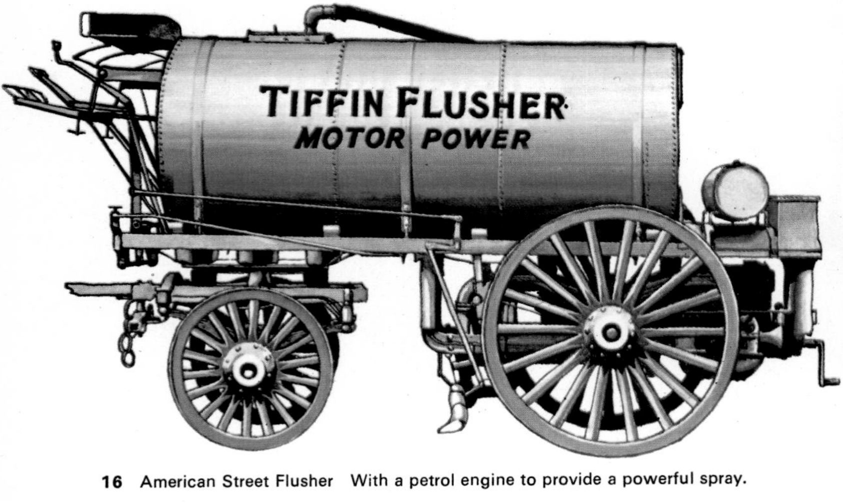

16 American Street Flusher With a petrol engine to provide a powerful spray.

17 American Mail Cart One of the many varieties of US Mail Cart in use during the early part of this century.

18 American Dump Wagon Bottom dumping wagon of exceptionally strong contruction. Rear axle is set well back and arched to avoid fouling of dumped load.

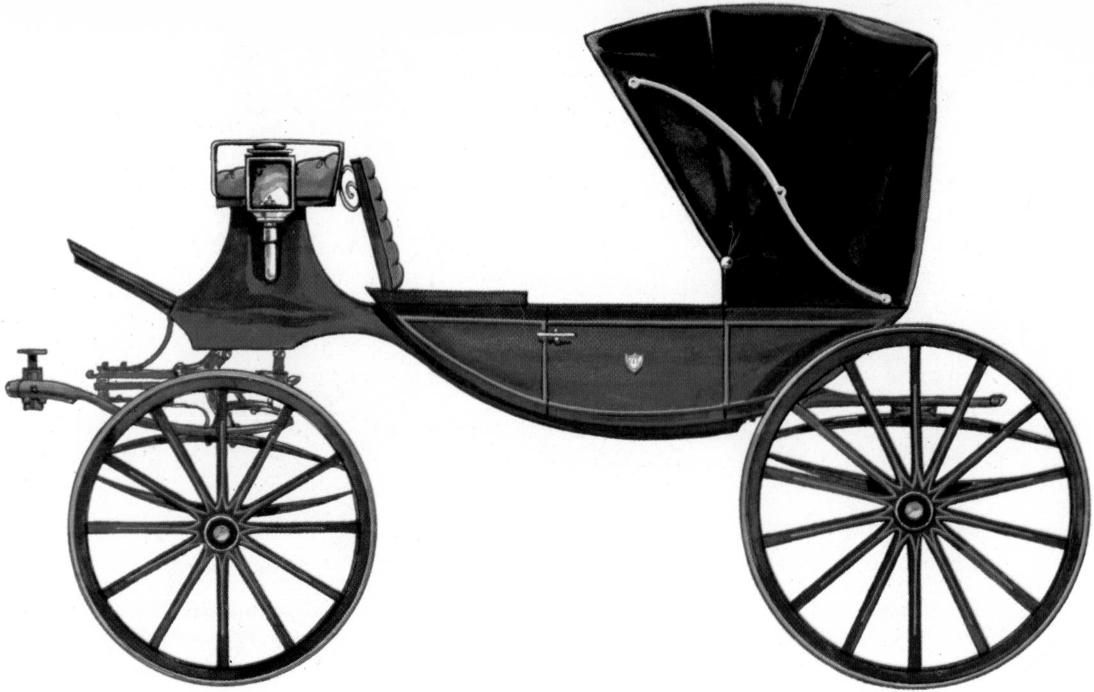

19 British Barouche The shallow body with sweeping bottom curve gives this carriage its elegant line. Large hood gives rear seat passengers ample protection from the rain.

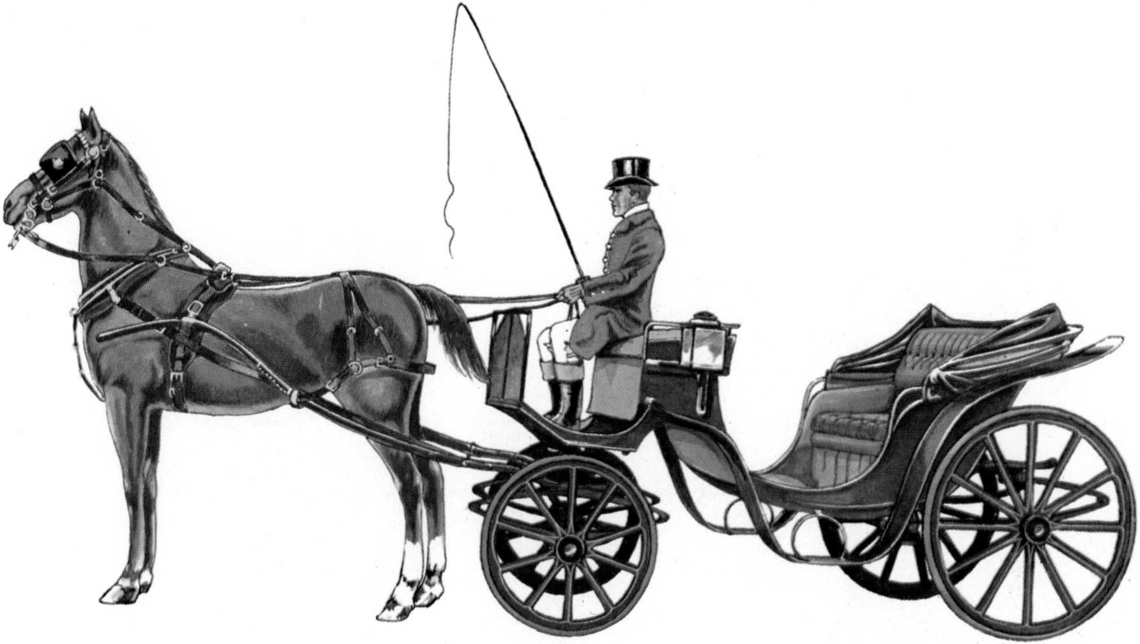

20 American Victoria A smart showground turnout is this north American version of the popular European carriage named after the long reigning British Queen. Low sweep of body provides ease of entry and gives bystanders an uninterrupted view of occupants.

21 American Phaeton The north American version of a very old style of vehicle taking its name from the Greek figure who is said to have driven his carriage too near to the sun.

22 American Fringe Top Surrey The pretty, popular almost legendary vehicle of North America. This model is on the older reach undergear. The Surrey appeared in many variations.

23 American Depot Wagon Another very popular style used as daily transport by many

24 American Rockaway North American style of popular road coach.

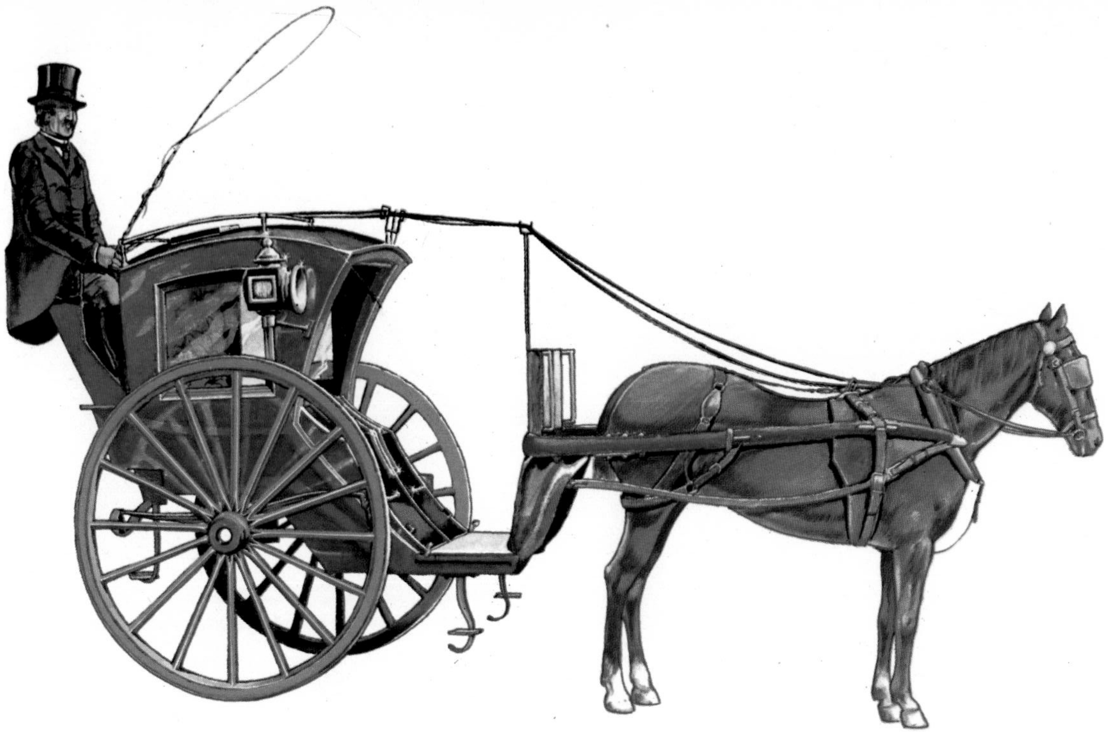

25 British Hansom Cab The basic style of vehicle to bear the name of its originator although differing somewhat from his first design.

26 British State Landau Seen here in its closed form the double hoods could be folded down to produce a most elegant carriage suitable for state occasions.

YORK
LONDON
MAIL
GR

27 British Mail Coach Once the fastest regular vehicles on British roads the mail coaches plied between major towns and cities carrying the Royal Mails.

28 Australian Mail Coach Based originally on American Concord coaches the first Cobb & Co coaches began service in 1854. Later vehicles locally built. Services subsequently started in South Africa.

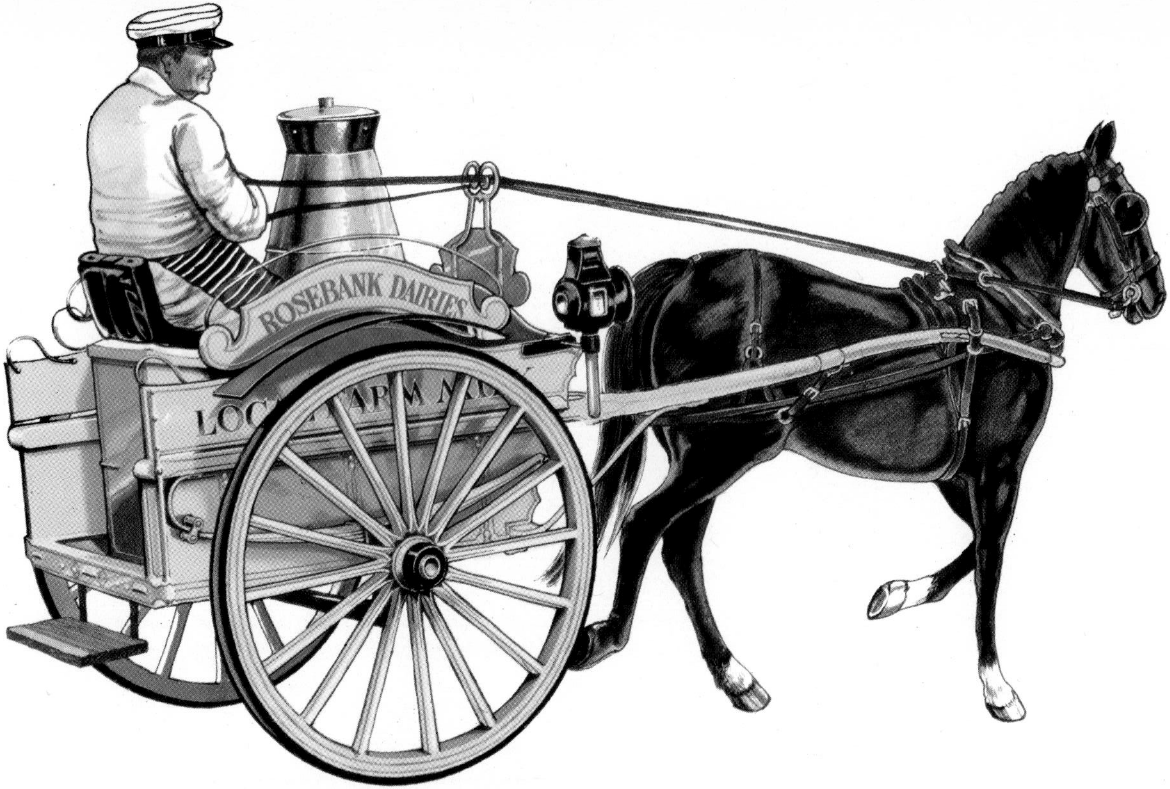

29 British Dairy Float The most popular style of milk float in the days when milk was dispensed from a large churn. Larger vehicles were introduced when the heavy bottles and crates came into use.

30 British Butcher's Cart Light type of cart for local deliveries. This style also found limited use in Australia.

31 American Fish Delivery Van Side panel is typical of the high quality painting and lettering of vehicles used by local tradesmen.

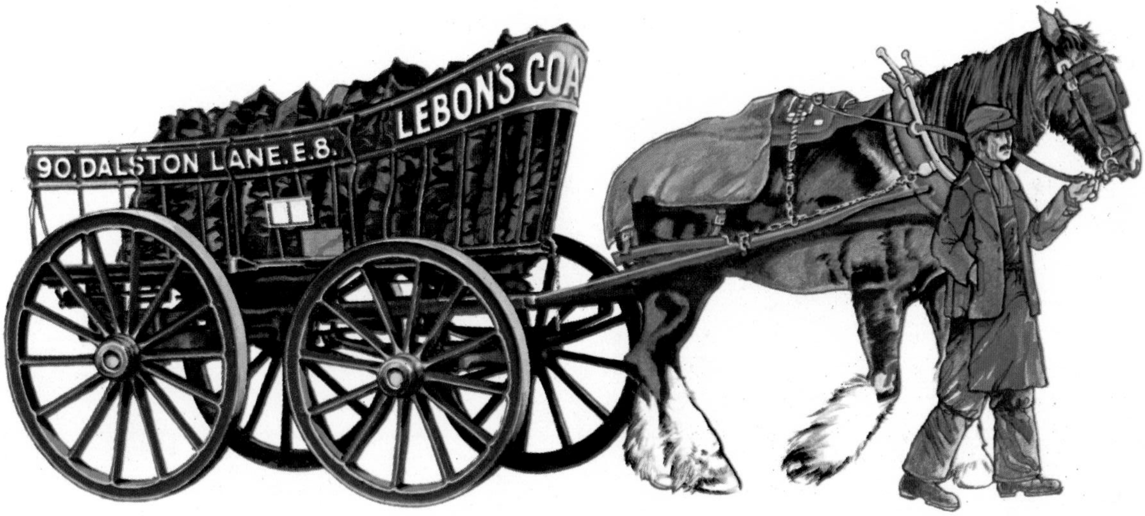

32 British Coal Van London style of bow fronted coal van used to carry the long and narrow coal sacks common in the south. Large front wheels demand a large turning area. Weighing scales stowed under rear of vehicle.

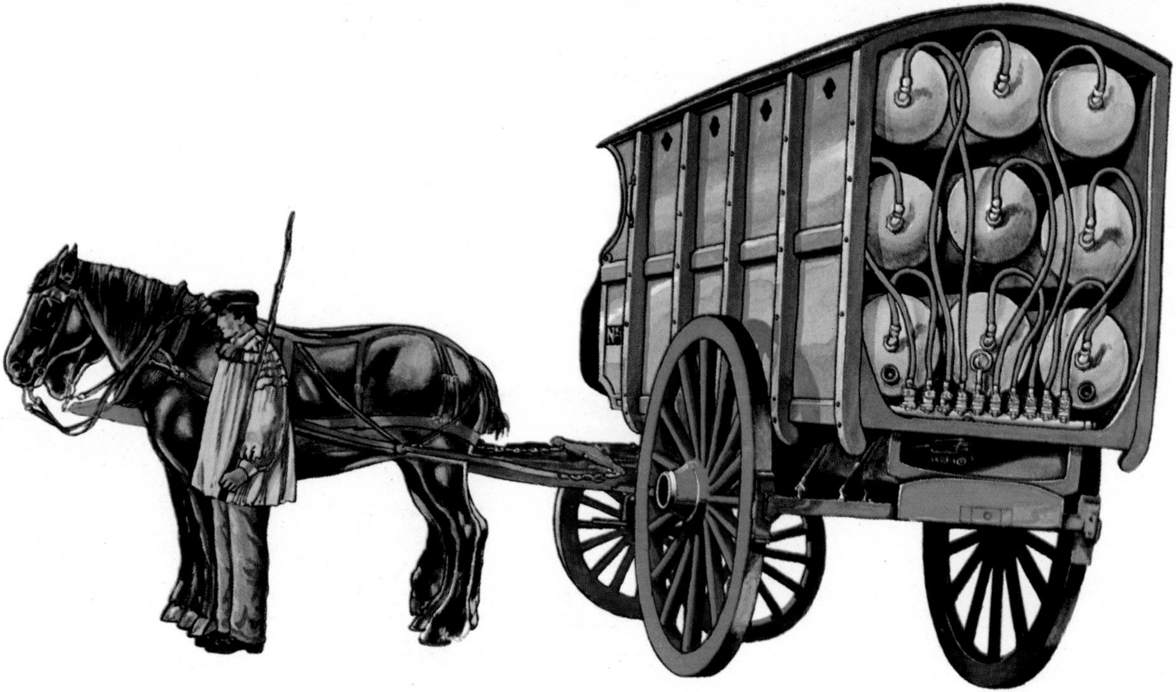

33 French Bulk Gas Van Unusual arrangement of cylinders in a van for the delivery of town gas in bulk to users on the outskirts of Paris who were not connected to the main supply.

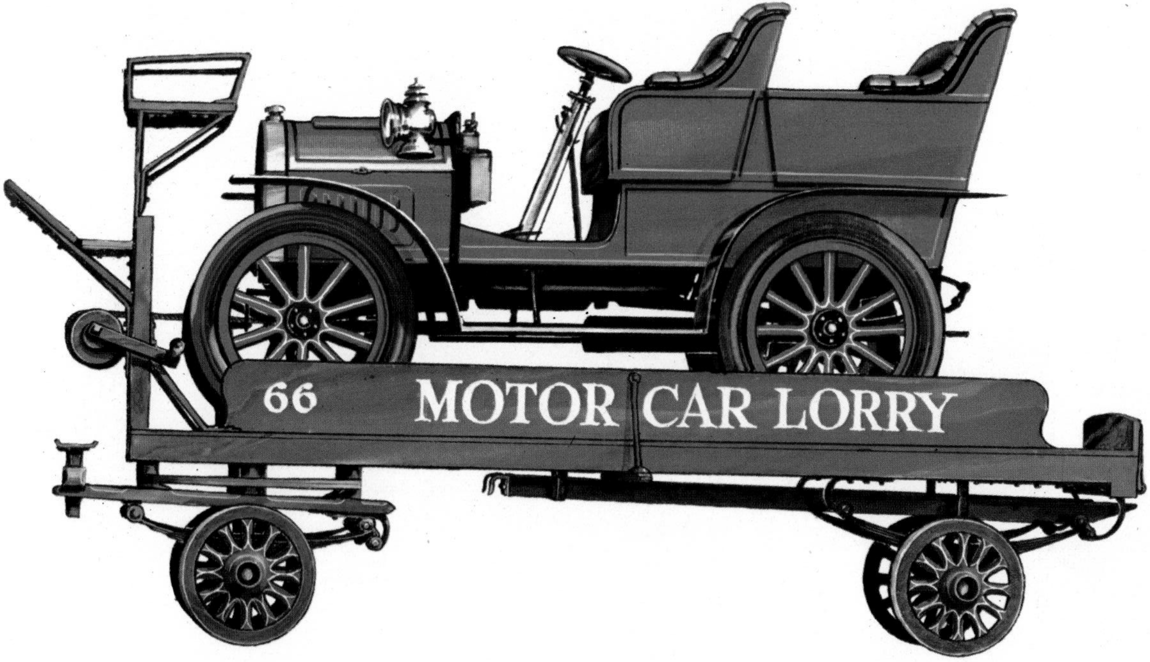

34 British Motor Car Lorry Special low loading vehicle for the movement of motor cars to railway depots or docks. Earlier designs for the transport of horse carriages were of lighter construction.

35 American Garbage Truck Boston style of garbage collection in demountable metal bins. Vehicle featured one step loading and lids to bins to keep out flies.

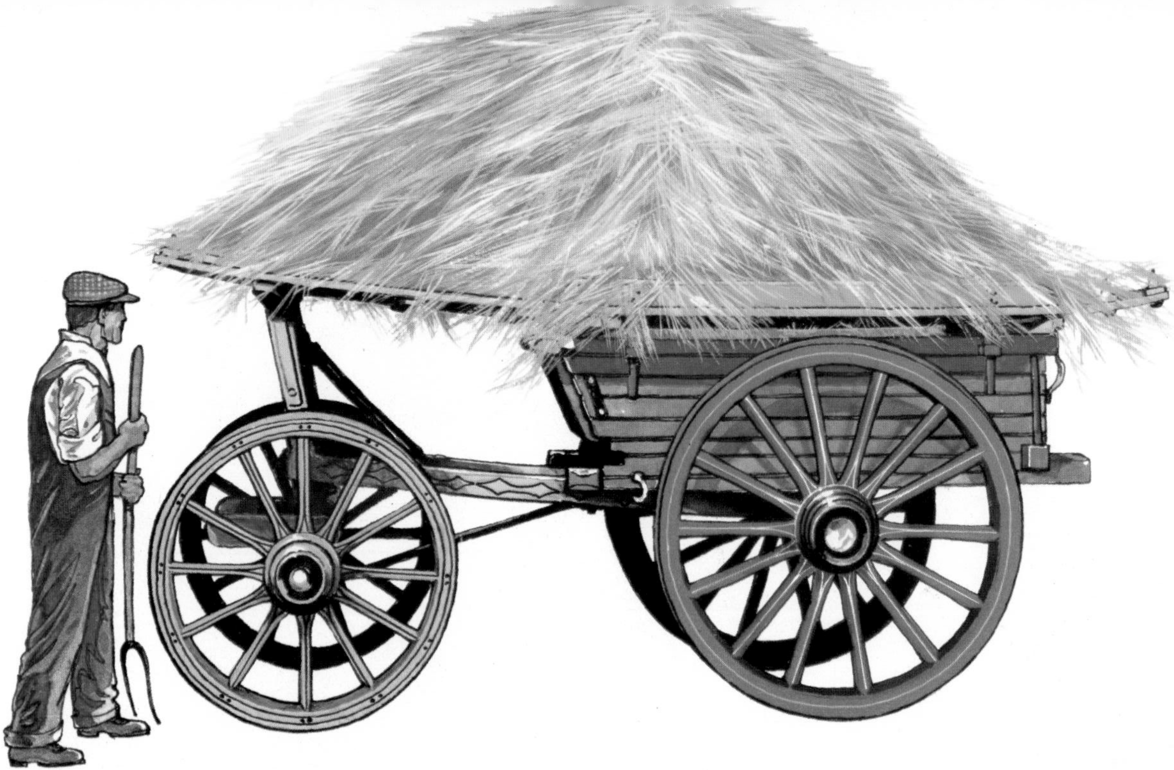

36 British Hermaphrodite Ingenious harvest time adaptation of a two wheeled cart for greater capacity.

37 Chinese Peking Cart Centuries old style of family or hired cart for passenger travel.

38 British Double Deck Omnibus Typical London 'garden seat' style of double decker seating twenty-eight passengers and averaging 7-8 m.p.h. in normal service. Name derived from type of seats placed crosswise on upper deck.

39 British Private Omnibus A development from the wagonette brake. Used for private parties, sporting events, etc. Also found wide use as hotel buses, station buses and latterly as public buses on rural routes.

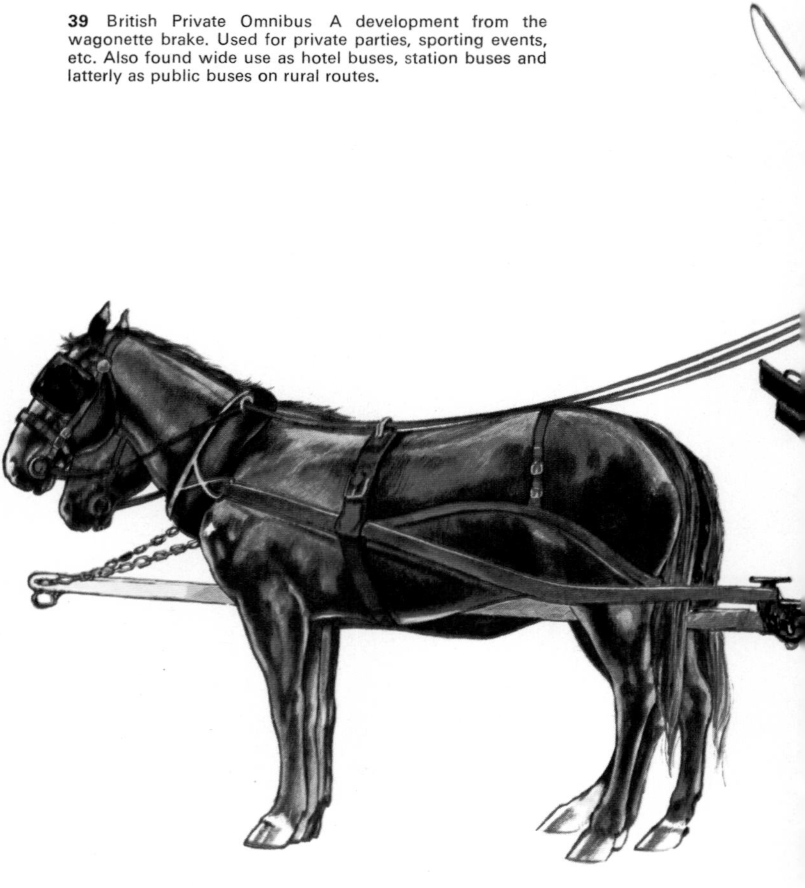

40 British Romany Caravan A Reading type of romany or gypsy caravan beautifully decorated. Other styles were the ledge type, the Burton, the bow top and the open lot.

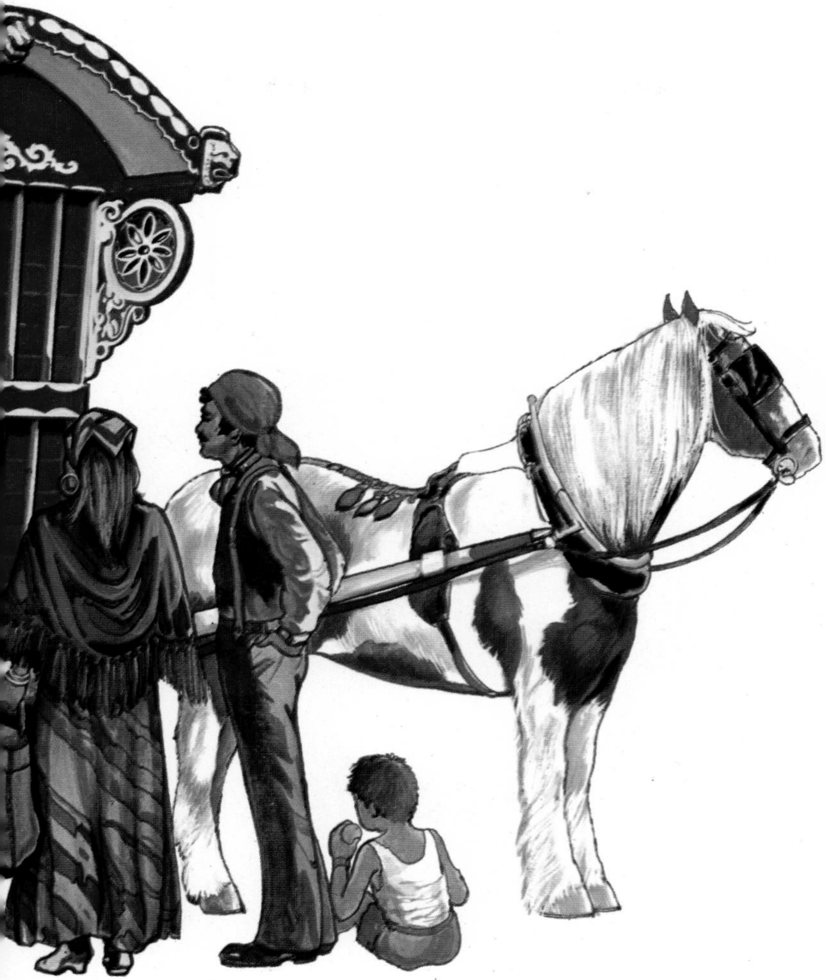

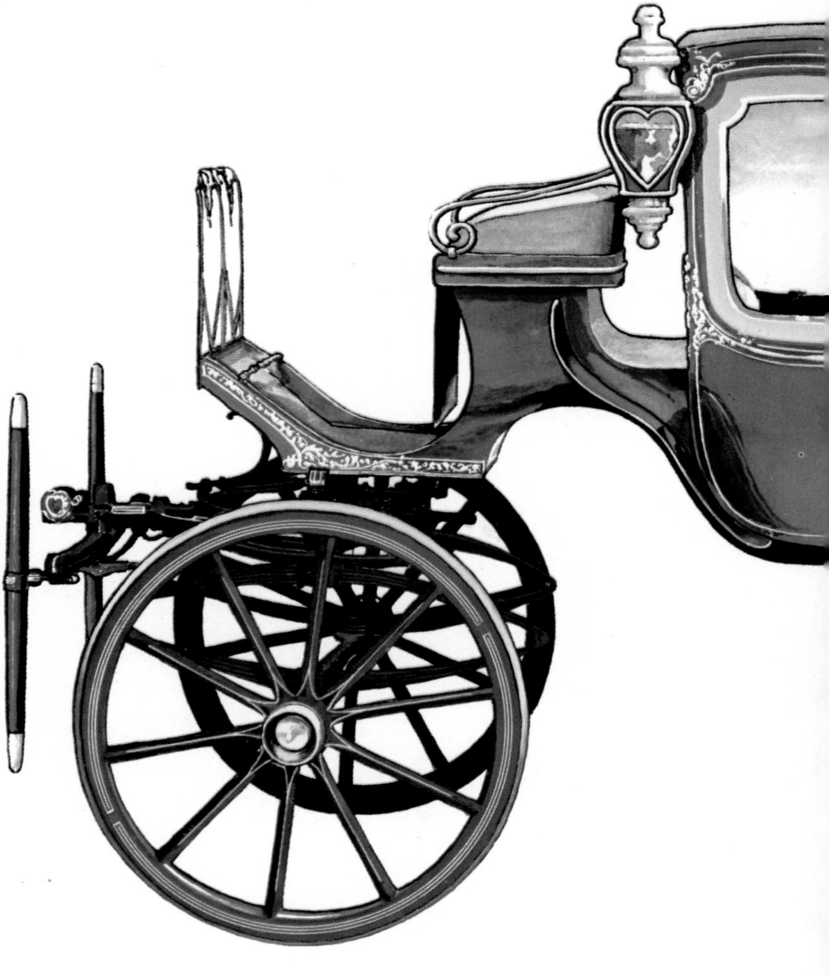

41 American Bridal Coach Fine carving, silver plating and heart shape motifs give this coach delicate refinement for the special occasion.

42 Swiss Diligence Catering for a large number of passengers and their luggage for long distance journeys this vehicle was the stage coach of Europe. Piles of luggage and goods were stowed on roof.

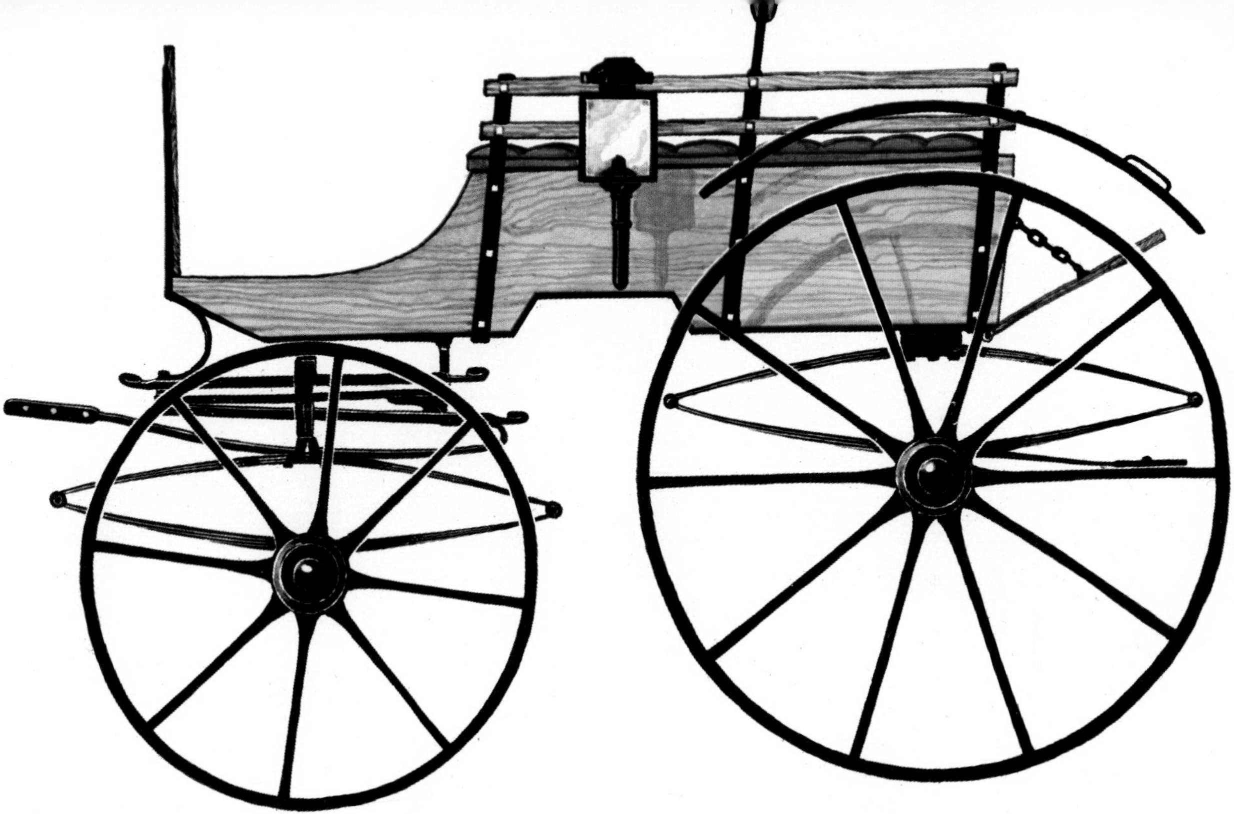

43 French Derby Cart Stark simplicity and basic economy was the hallmark of this vehicle.

44 British Trailer Dustcart A combination trailer dustcart which could be drawn by a horse in shafts for house to house collection and by a motor tractive unit for longer journeys.

45 British Brewer's Dray One of the trade show turnouts.

46 American Florist's Van An elegant glass panelled van which displays its colourful load while its equally elegant driver steps out to make a delivery.

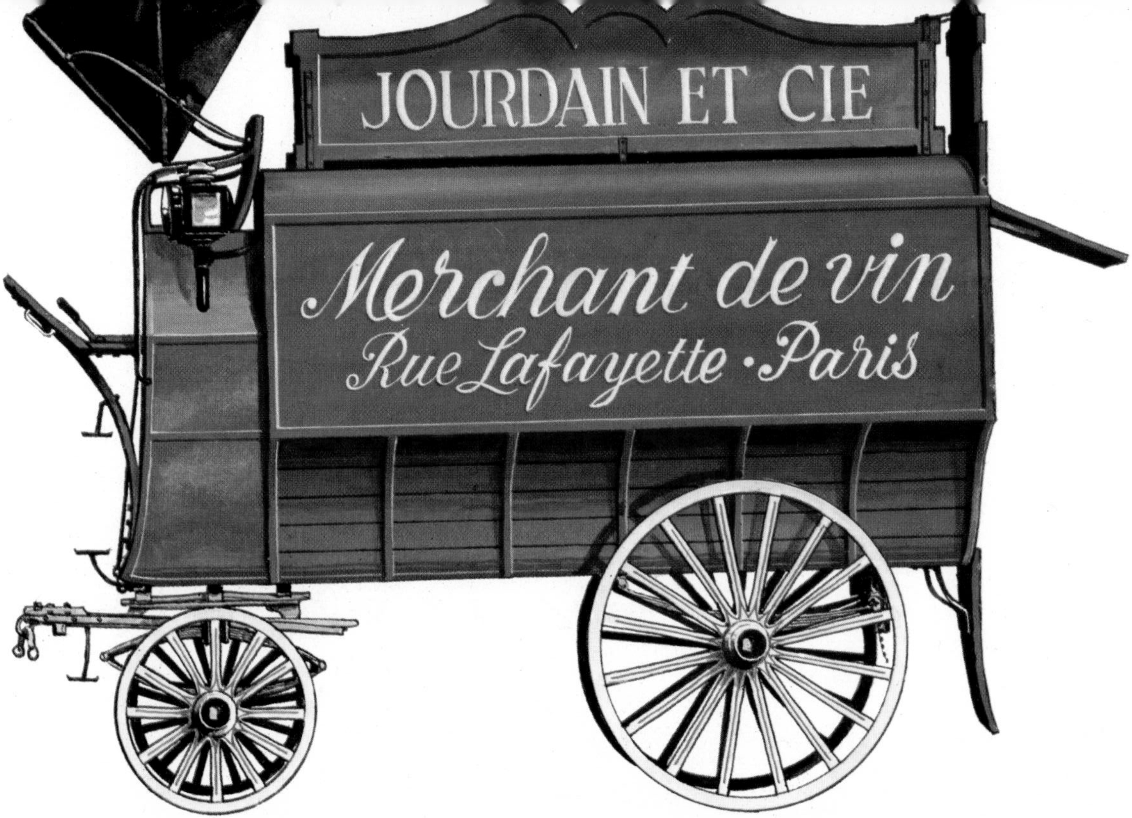

47 French Wine Van   Displaying its Parisian design by way of its quality panelling

49 British Living Van A very substantial transportable home with facilities for a comfortable existence whether used for site work or pleasure.

50 American Buggy The personal transport of countless thousands of pre-motor era Americans. Some were more simply made than this example which has a comfortable well upholstered seat and four bow hood.

51 British Brougham One of the more well-known types of horse-drawn carriage taking its name from the first avid user, the Lord Brougham.

52 British Char-à-banc Of French origin, the larger types provided economical transport for thousands of day-trippers and holidaymakers to the country or seaside.

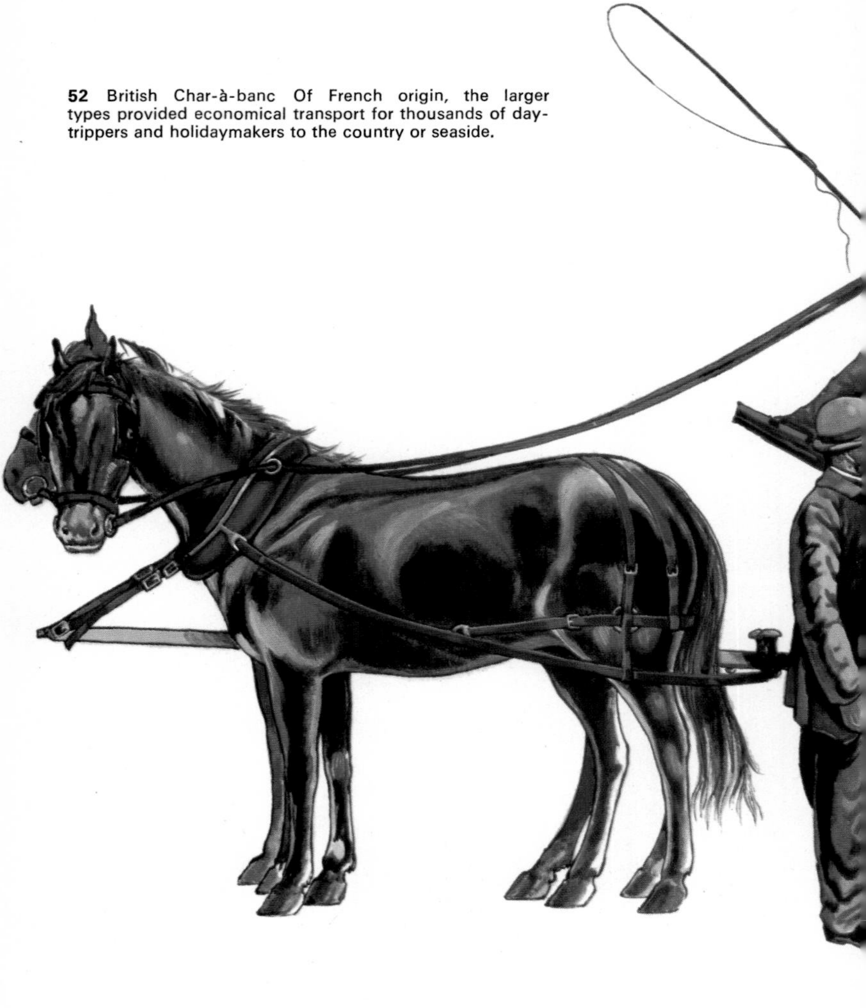

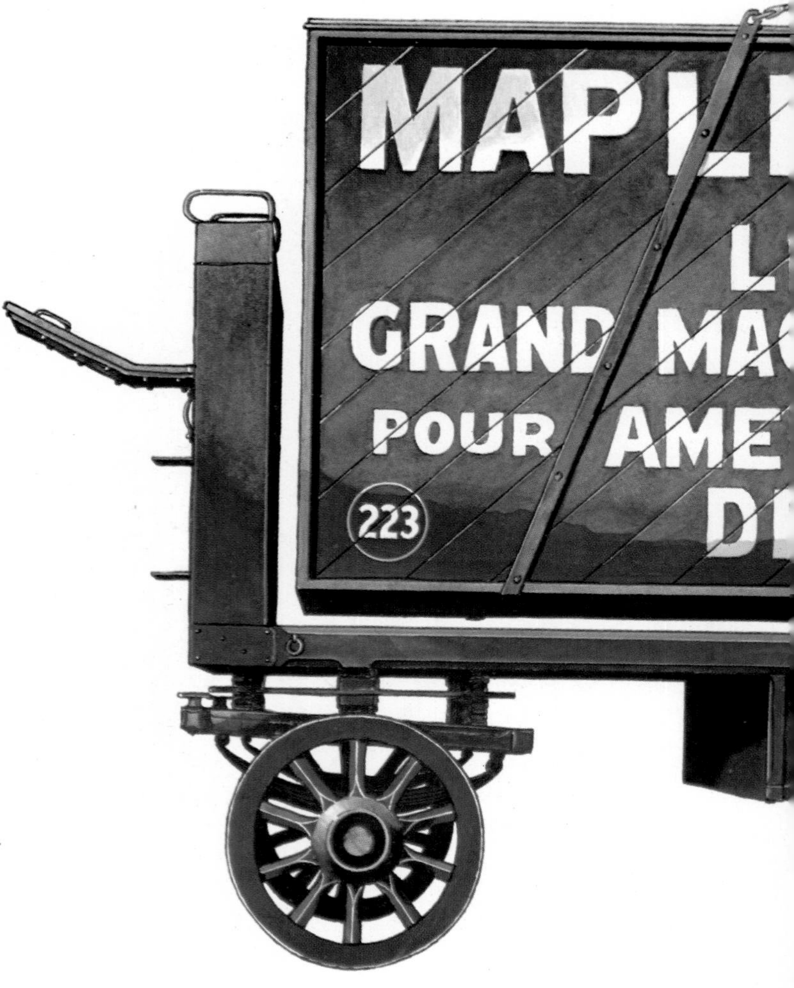

53 British Trolley and Lift Van The business of overseas removals benefitted from the introduction of lift vans. The well beneath the floor of the trolley was useful for stowing packing materials.

CIE LONDRES
ET PARIS
PLUS
IN DE L'UNIVERS
LEMENT
RATION
By Appointment
to H.M. the King

54 American Steam Fire Engine Nothing could match the sheer excitement of the powerful steam fire engines belching fire and smoke as the two or three horses galloped away from the fire department.

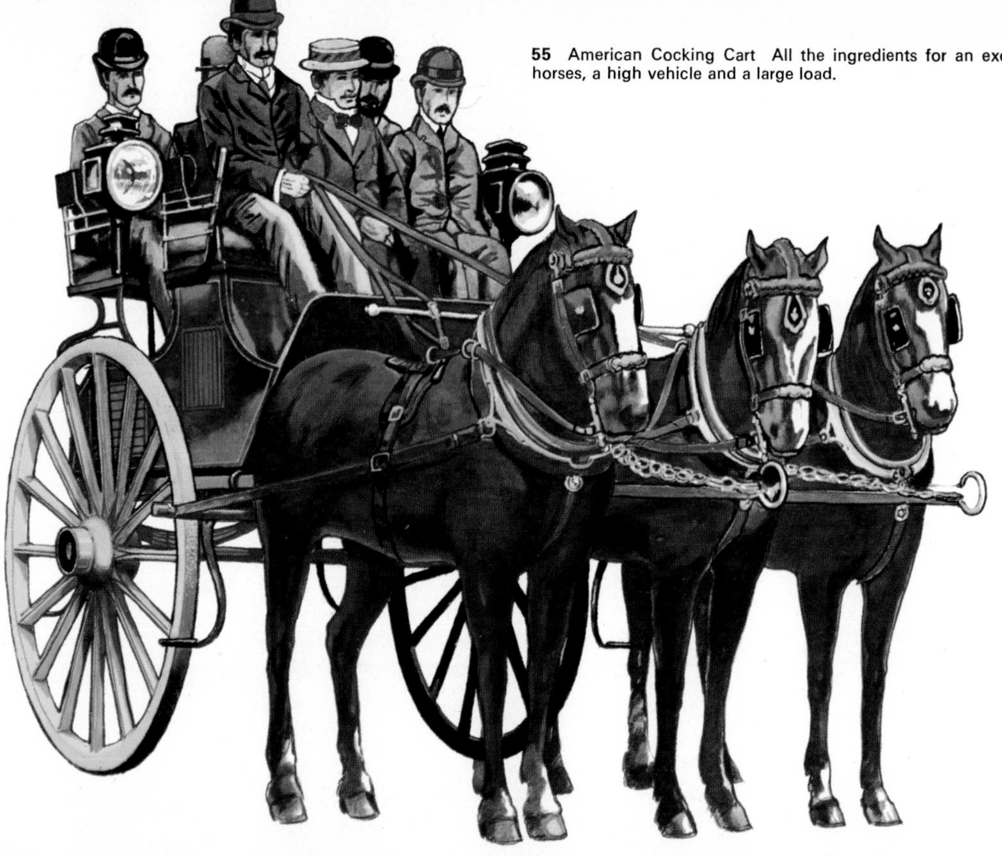

55 American Cocking Cart All the ingredients for an exciting drive – three fast horses, a high vehicle and a large load.

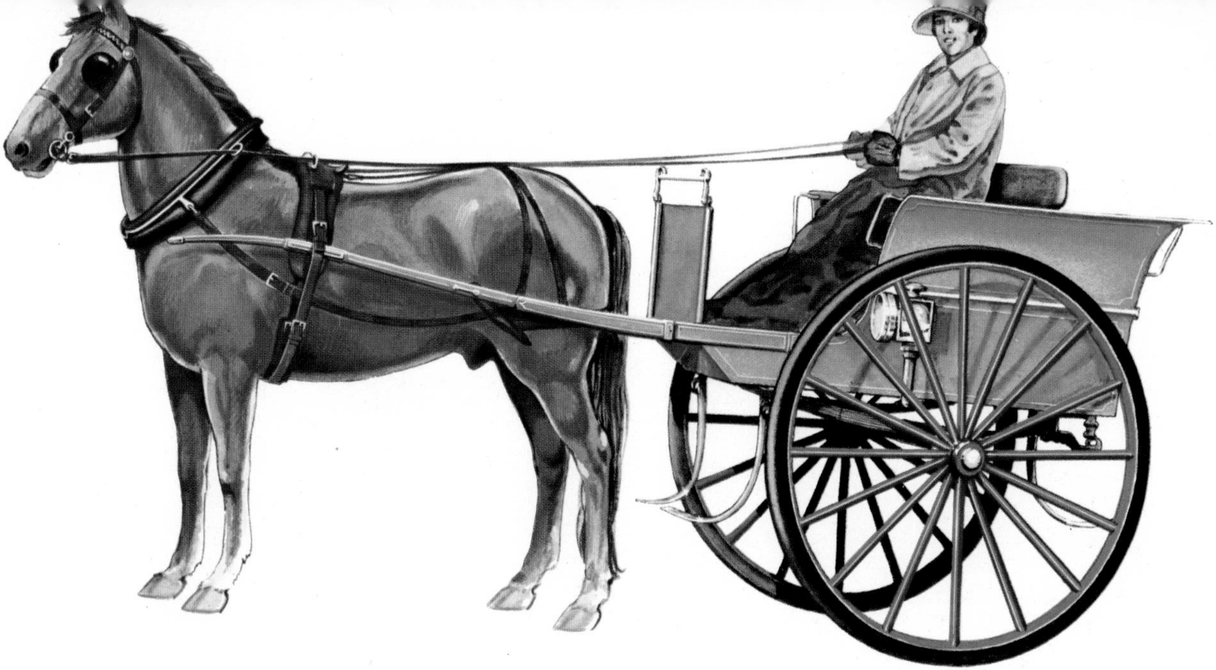

56 British Ralli Car The nicely radiused side panels curve out to form wheel splashers and the shafts are placed within the body to form the basic points of the Ralli or Driving Car.

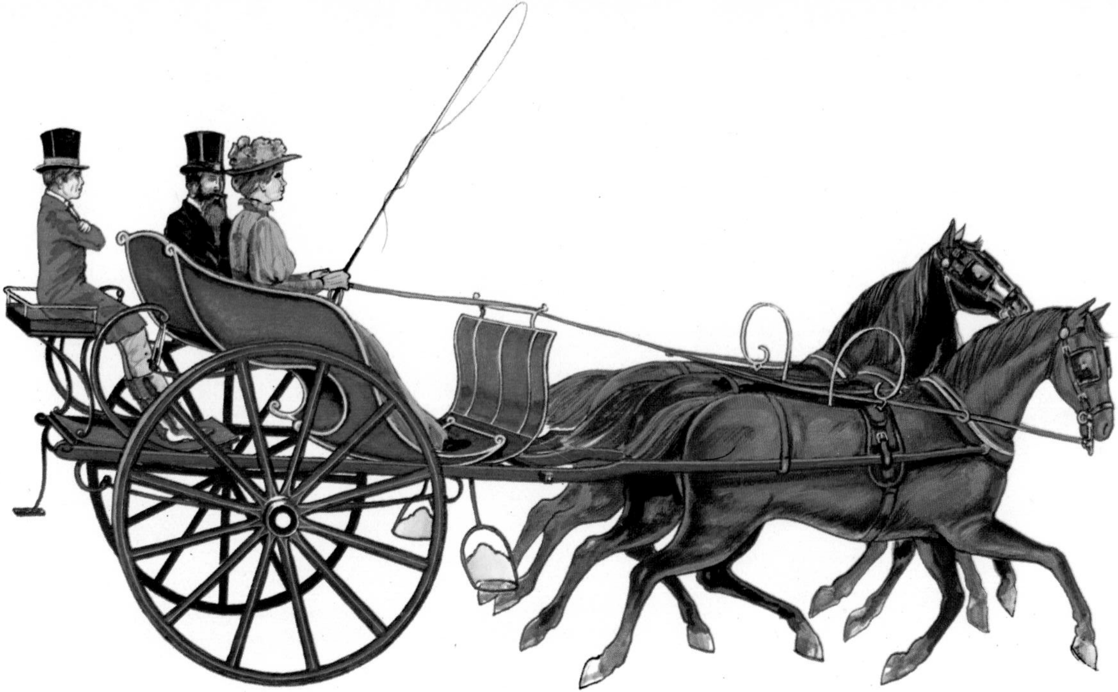

57 British Troika Curricle Once thought to be the height of fashion, an elegantly curved body and dasher, tiny 'tiger' at the rear and three horses abreast 'troika fashion'.

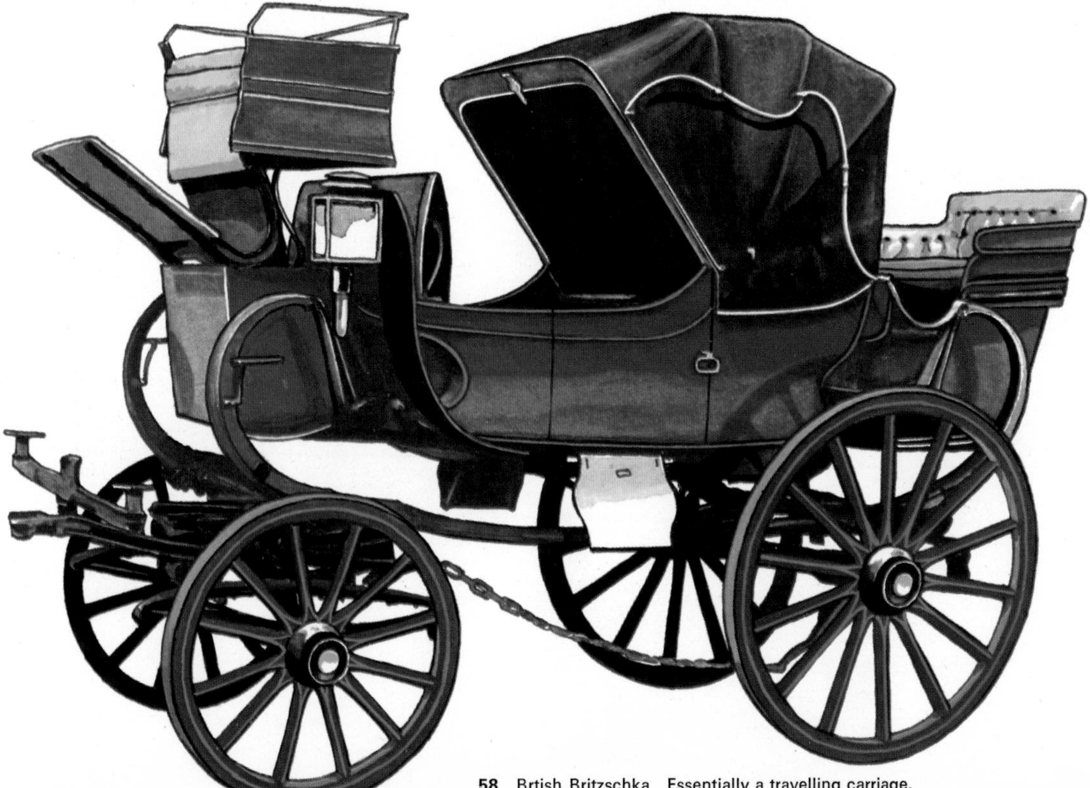

58 Brtish Britzschka   Essentially a travelling carriage.

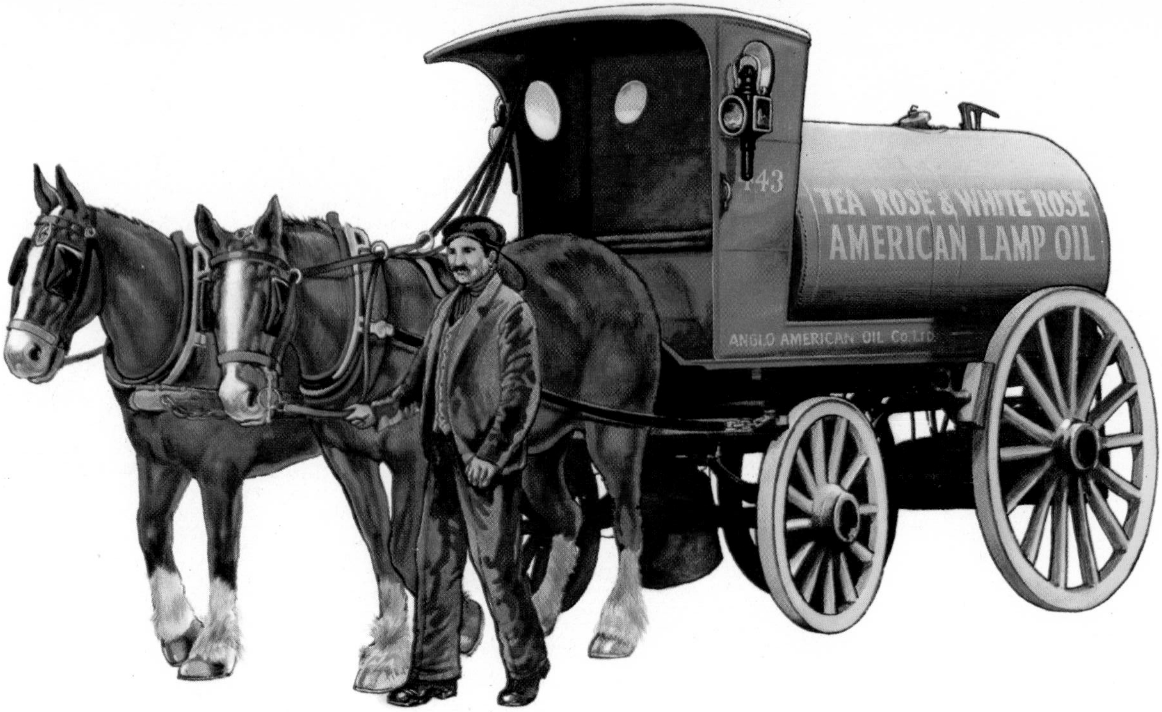

59 British Paraffin Tanker Paraffin (kerosene) tankers like this collected the oil from the rail depot and delivered it to shops and houses.

METROPOLITAN RAILWAY.
62
FARRINGDON St. GOODS DEPOT. EC

61 British Ragman's Trolley Still to be found in the streets of some large towns although not collecting rags since the introduction of man made fibres. Today its load is more likely to be scrap iron or junk.

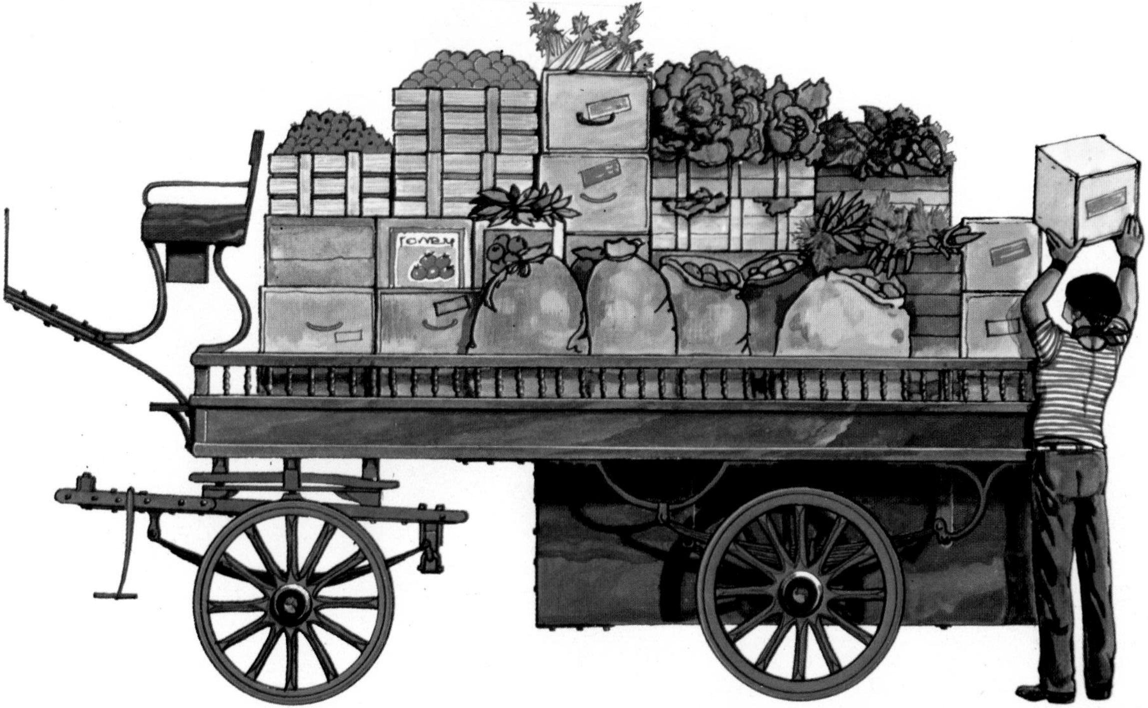

62 French Produce Van A cranked axle and well floor provide ample space for a load of fruit and vegetables on this market trader's van with attractive railed sides.

63 American Moving Van Attractive and clever use of the large van sides leaves no doubt as to the resourcefulness of this remover.

64 American Gospel Wagon The organist plays a few bars, the preacher welcomes the choristers and the first of the congregation gather before the church on wheels.

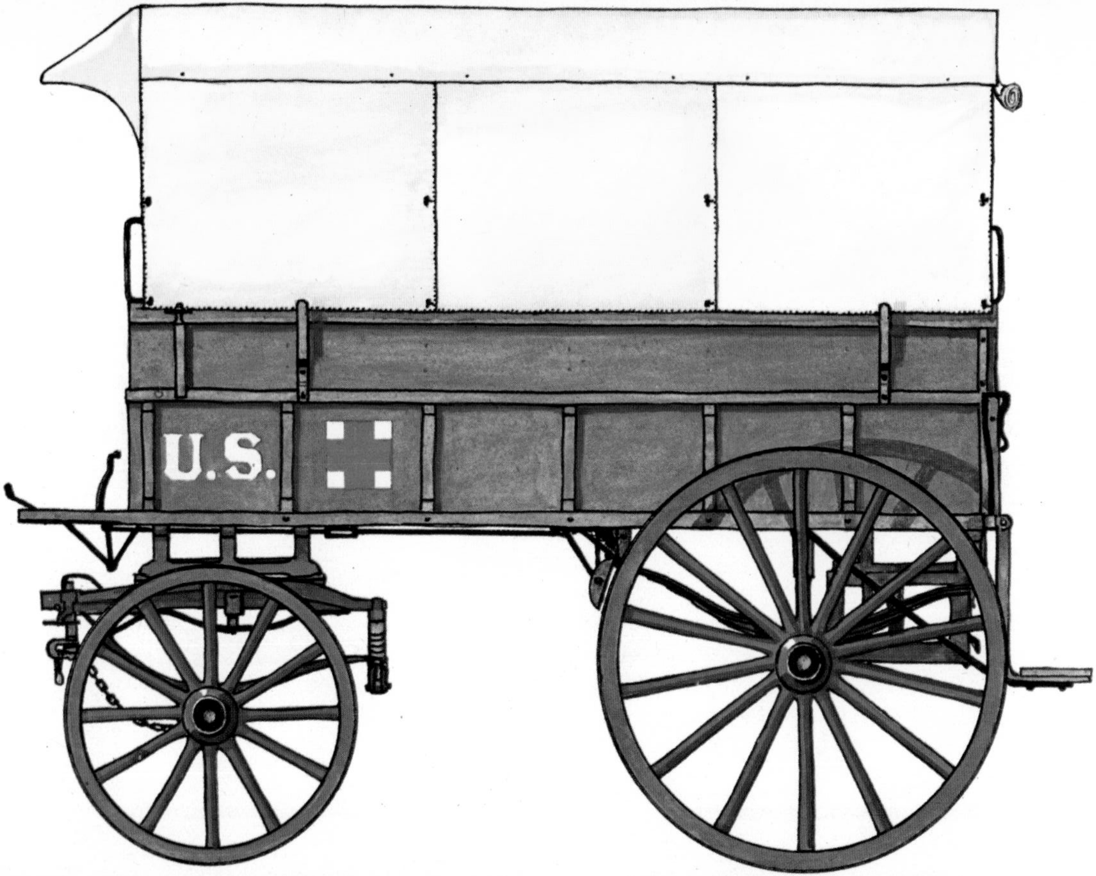

65 American Army Ambulance. Takes both sitting and stretcher cases

66 British Funeral Hearse Typical style of hearse featuring large glass panels and silver fittings as a relief from the sombre all black boxes of earlier designs.

67 American Circus Band Wagon All the gaiety and excitement of the big top is represented in this magnificent wagon which conveys the circus band.

68 German Brewer's Dray To obviate the need to lift the beer casks very high, part of this dray's load is carried slung from the chains beneath the vehicle body.

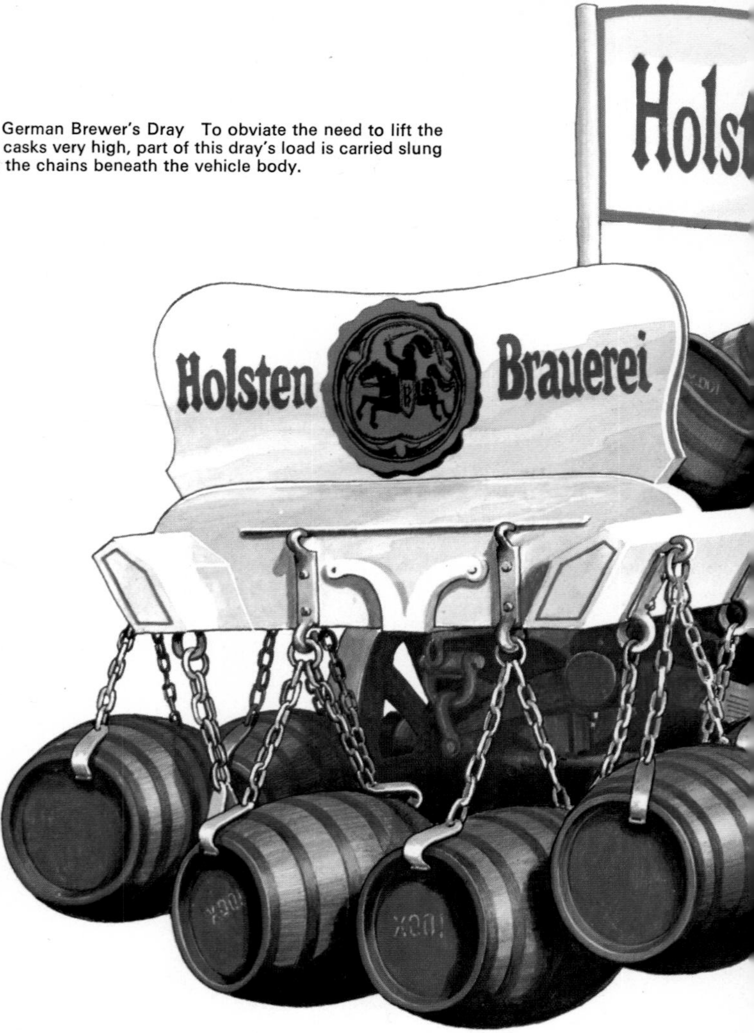

Bier
TEN BRAUEREI

69 American Police Patrol This was the style of vehicle used to carry the drunks and rowdies back to the jailhouse.

POLICE

70 American Ice Van Style of ice van favoured in the Philadelphia area. Type of vehicle used varied according to level of summer temperature.

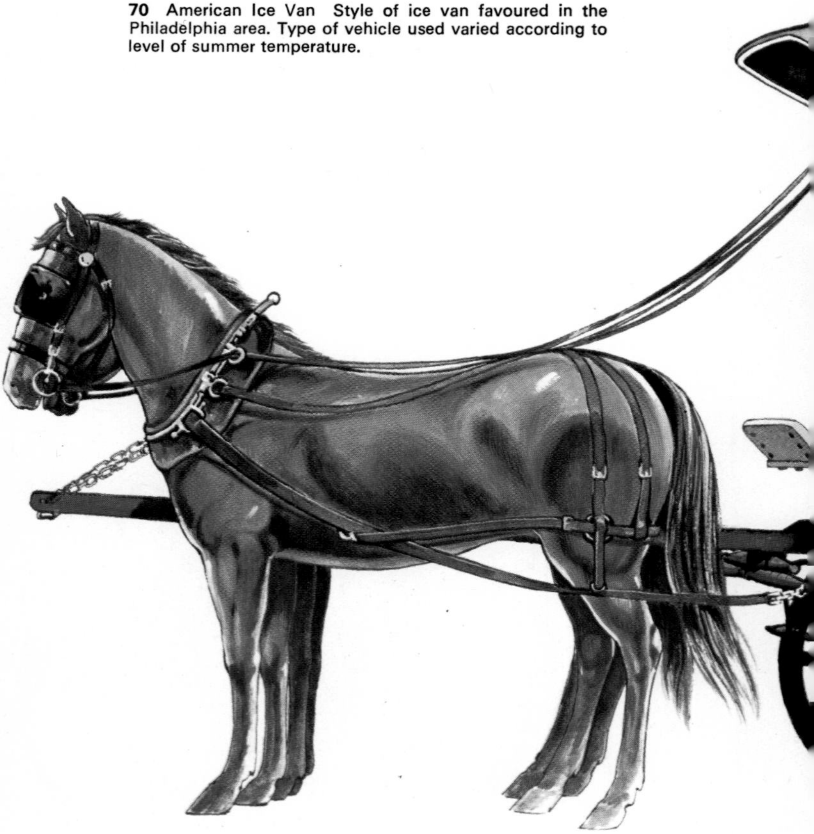

PEOPLES'
ICE

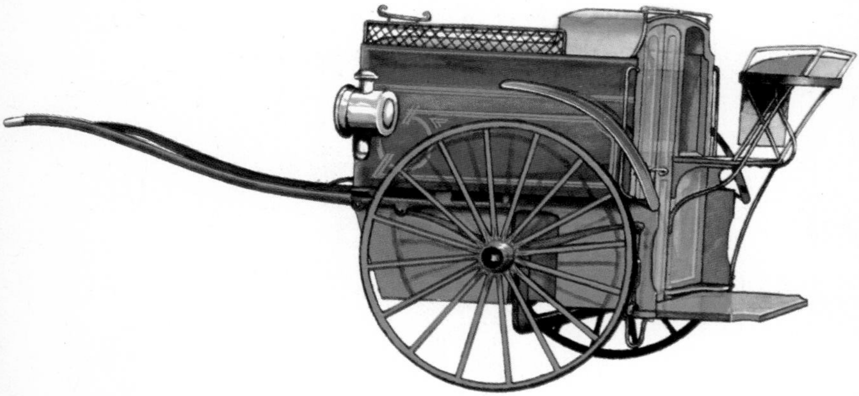

71 American Light Trade Cart Style of light delivery cart used by some city tradespeople. Type bears some resemblance to British tradesmen's carts.

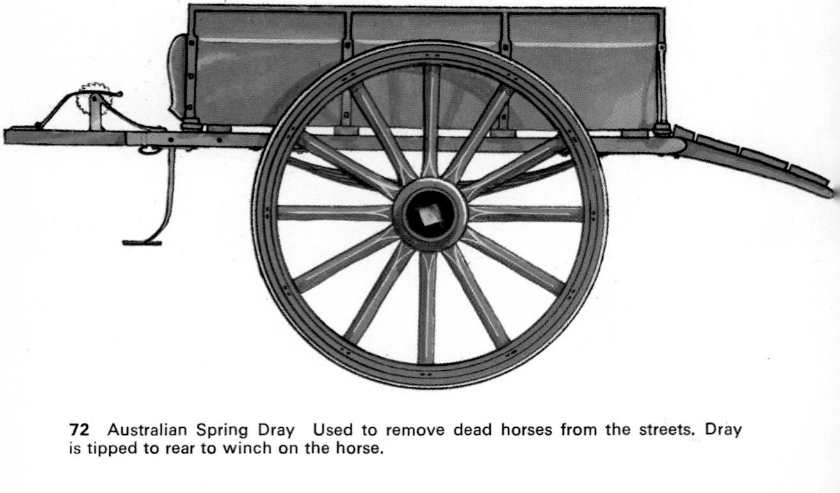

72 Australian Spring Dray Used to remove dead horses from the streets. Dray is tipped to rear to winch on the horse.

THE PLATE DESCRIPTIONS

Irish Outside Car *Plate 1*

If one had to list the types of vehicle which are representative of certain countries there is no doubt that upon arriving at Ireland it would be that unique style shown in our illustration, to be sure!

The jaunting car or to give it its proper title the Irish outside car certainly was a type which found a great following both for private use and as a Hackney cab. It could be procured just with the two outside facing seats and in this case the driver sat to one side at an angle. To provide seats for four passengers a separate, forward facing seat for the driver could be added, and when the vehicle was required for private use some coachbuilders provided a rearward facing seat for a servant.

Cars for private use were often much better finished than the Hackney variety being furnished with leather dash, wings etc. and better quality upholstery, plated fittings and lamps.

A typical specification for an outside car is as follows:

Overall length including shafts	9 ft 7 in.
,, width over steps	6 ft 10 in.
,, height	4 ft 11 in.
Length of side seat	3 ft 0 in.
Height of wheels	3 ft 0 in.

Length of springs	4 ft 0 in.
Track	3 ft 9 in.

Another style of vehicle peculiar to Ireland was the Irish stage coaches introduced by Bianconi, these being really an enlarged version of the outside car and carried on four wheels.

Removal Van *Plate 2*

Furniture removal vans or pantechnicons were generally made in three main sizes termed small, medium and large and were usually between 12 ft and 18 ft in length. Basically they were a rectangular box shape of large cubic capacity in order to stow as much furniture as possible. A sharply radiused roof was provided to ensure that rain was quickly discharged; access was by means of a large pair of hinged doors at the rear and the driver's seat was positioned somewhere at the front usually high up if not actually on the roof.

In order to make use of the full body width of 7 ft the wheels were of small diameter and positioned below the floor line or if larger rear wheels were used then semi-circular recesses were provided within the sides of the body to accommodate them. These arches or paddle boxes needed only to be 5 inches deep so not much of the interior capacity was used.

Early types of van had a flat floor but after a Mr Purdy had successfully produced his style with the well in the floor and supported on a cranked rear axle, many vans were of this improved type.

Because of their immense size for the day the large flat sides and rear were put to good use in advertising the owner's name, address, business, area of operations and almost anything else you care to mention. Unlike today when many large van sides are completely devoid of any message save perhaps for a meaningless logo the vans of yesteryear looked like a travelling hoarding and were a tribute to the skill of the lettering artist. Not that it finished there. Many vans had deep boards bolted to the outside edges of the roof so that additional boxes, trunks and other light articles could be carried on the roof and these boards often carried the old familiar cliches of 'removals to all parts', 'distance no object' or 'branches in all large towns'.

One particular feature of some of the vans was the painting of scenes along the sides. Often there were pictures of rolling countryside with a removal van trundling through the picture taking some happy household to a new home. After the railways came along to cream the long distance transport market the removal vans could be seen roped down on railway 'carriage trucks' and being whisked to far off destinations much quicker than the horse teams. This was the original piggyback concept and was very suitable for the railways so as to achieve a co-ordinated road/rail system as long as the vans were within the loading gauge.

To return to the vans themselves, a look through a typical specification reveals that a medium sized van of 16 ft overall length was 6 ft 8 in. wide and 4 ft 8 in. high from floor. The well was 9 ft 8 in. long and 4 ft 8 in. wide. The van was carried on 2 ft 8 in. front wheels and 4 ft 2 in. rear wheels with springs of 3 ft 4 in. at the front and 3 ft 8 in. at the rear. The rear axle was cranked to a depth of 1 ft 5 in.

The roof had a radius of 8 in. and the roof boards were 1 ft high. The back was enclosed by double doors and outside of these was a substantially made drop tailboard hinged at the bottom of the well. In point of fact this tailboard was a useful load carrier and often used for a wardrobe or chest of drawers suitably protected from the elements by a sheet and roped to top and sides.

The practical use of these vans is borne out by the fact that very many outlived the horse teams by many years. With the advent of the steam traction engine or road locomotive the vans underwent a new lease of life often being towed two or three at a time. Some removers found that the later paraffin and petrol engine tractors could still utilize the old horse vans and so they enjoyed another reprieve, often finishing their days mounted on rubber tyred wheels being towed as trailers behind the Leyland, Dennis or Saurer petrol vans of the 1920's.

Gold State Coach *Plate 3*

The Gold State Coach still to be seen in the Royal Mews at Buckingham Palace dates from 1762 and has been used by the reigning monarchs for coronations and most openings of Parliament since that time.

Like most other State coaches it is a large and cumbersome vehicle weighing around 4 tons and measuring some 24 ft long, 8 ft 3 in. wide and 12 ft high overall. There is a vast amount of gilding on the coach and the pictures on the panels are attributed to the Florentine painter Cipriani.

The design of the coach is by Sir William Chambers but there is no record of who built it. It is most elaborately decorated and has all the carved figures and insignia in the true tradition of a royal carriage. The coach body framing is carved to represent eight palm trees and these branch out at their tops to form supports for the roof, in the centre of which are carved three cherubs who support the royal crown and hold various state symbols in their hands.

The coach is suspended on leather braces held by four life size carved figures and the driver's footboard is a large scallop shell supported on bundles of reeds.

Eight horses are used to draw the coach which was originally driven by a coachman from the box plus one postillion, but in later years the driver's box was removed and the coach put under the control of four postillions.

Cabriolet *Plate 4*

Because of its name it is supposed that the cabriolet originated in France somewhere in the seventeenth century and Count Gozzadini in his work on ancient carriages says they were introduced into Italy in 1672. He described this early design as being like a gig with a curving body mounted on two long shafts with a pair of wheels at the opposite end to the horse. G. A. Thrupp thought that this type of vehicle may have been the origin of vehicles in various parts of the world such as the carriole of Norway, the calesso of Naples and the volante of Cuba. When it arrived in England it had a small shell like body covered with a small folding hood and containing a small seat.

Naturally the design underwent changes during its life span and cabriolets of the nineteenth century were not unlike a curricle or gig. Generally speaking they were for one or two persons only protected by a folding leather hood over the seat and a high curved dasher at the front. The elegantly curved body was pitched just within the curved shafts which terminated at the rear in C-springs and leather braces, with a small platform at the rear for the footman.

Another variation of the cabriolet was that of producing a four wheel version and as privately driven four wheelers were known as phaetons the new design was called a cabriolet phaeton or cab phaeton for short. The name cab had been coined earlier in fact through the action of a coachbuilder David Davies who in 1823 had put the first licensed 'Hackney Cabriolets' on the London streets. These were the two wheeled variety of cabriolet with a separate seat for the driver.

Dog Cart *Plate 5*

The dog cart depicted in this illustration took its name from the fact that it was a special vehicle derived from the gig family and used for carrying dogs. It was really two seats placed back to back over a box to hold the sporting pointers or fast greyhounds and ventilation was by means of Venetian slats at both sides of the box. The rear seat passengers were provided with a footboard and the box opened under their feet to get at the dogs.

Variations came in the way of making the box or boot larger, raising the driver's seat and that of the groom on iron-work and driving the vehicle to a tandem pair – hence the name tandem cart.

Other varieties of the dog cart took their names from various sources according to circumstances; the Whitechapel with its open railed sides was so-called because of its origin as a trade cart in that part of London. The Oxford, Manchester, Newport and Bedford were also named after the areas in which they had their origins. Minor variations were numerous and included details such as boot shape, springing, seat shape and possibly use. They were used by all sorts of people in both town and country areas, but particularly by country dwellers.

The ralli car had its origins in the dog cart, but in this design the shafts were placed inside the body and pleasant outward curving boards were positioned over the wheels to prevent mud being thrown up on the passengers and children getting their hands in the spokes!

It was only natural that larger, four wheel versions of the dog cart would appear in due course and these were able to carry more in the way of passengers on the seats or parcels in the boot; they were usually driven to a pair in this size. To the purist there is no such thing as a four-wheeled cart and as soon as four wheels are put under a dog cart it becomes a phaeton, but that's just one point of view. Many of the later dog carts were never meant to carry dogs, so the Venetian slats at the sides were either sham ones just painted on or not even shown at all. Conversely the slats did give some relief to an otherwise plain expanse of boot or body so often other types of vehicle had Venetians be they on an English char-a-banc or an Australian city cart.

Bow Wagon *Plate 6*

The Australian farmer's Bow Wagon originated at Kyneton, Victoria, in the 1870's when a hay and corn dealer got a local wheelwright to construct a wagon to his design.

Vehicles with large strong wheels were usually built with high bodies and this made hard work of loading and unloading at ground level. If the floor of the vehicle was brought down to near axle height then the problem was reduced but then so was the usable capacity of the vehicle, it being limited to the space between the wheels.

So with the Bow Wagon a compromise was reached: the body was made low in the middle and the floor was extended out to the full width between the front and rear wheels and at the extreme rear, and then wide curving 'bows' were arranged over the wheels so that the total area was not diminished.

The principle was also adapted for two-wheel hay carts, in this instance the body being brought out to its full width both in front and behind the wheels.

In the four-wheel design shown in the illustration the principal dimensions are: 12 ft 4 in. overall length; 6 ft 9 in. overall width; 3 ft 7 in. floor height and height at top of bow 5 ft 7 in. The body summers are made out of 6 in. × $3\frac{1}{2}$ in. and finished with a sweep of about an inch on the top surface and tapering to about $2\frac{1}{2}$ in. at the ends. In plan they narrow about 8 in. at the front in order to allow the front axle to lock round slightly. The axle beds are of 6 in. × 6 in. and the bolsters 6 in. × 3 in. Floorboards were laid crossways and were 6 in. × $\frac{7}{8}$ in.

The bows over the wheels are made up of three parallel half round lengths of iron the ends of which are bolted to the widest part of the body namely the platforms at the extreme rear and between the sets of wheels. These platforms are constructed from three widths of 5 in. × 2 in. hardwood which extend the full width of the body. The front ends of the front bows are carried up to form the supports for the short hay ladder of 3 in. boards. Inside the bows are side boards measuring at front and rear 9¼ in. and 13½ in. respectively.

Farmer's Wagon *Plate 7*

This illustration shows a design of wagon which found use by thousands of American farmers, smallholders and other tradesmen in most parts of the United States. As stated elsewhere in this volume it is not the intention to include strictly agricultural vehicles as these fall into a separate category and are better dealt with on their own, but this type of wagon was produced all over and was more of a general utility vehicle than a farm wagon.

It was built on the most straightforward and simple of lines with just two small springs for the seat as a token of comfort. It had to be strong to withstand the incessant jolting of carrying loads over poor or non-existent roads; it had to be simple in construction to facilitate repair by unskilled hands, and it was well ironed to obviate the need for complicated joints without sacrificing strength.

Naturally each builder had his own ideas as to the size and arrangement of the wagon but a typical design is shown in our plate and the following details give the main dimensions:

Overall length	8 ft 6 in.
,, width	6 ft 0 in.
,, height	5 ft 5 in.
Front wheels	3 ft 4 in.
Rear wheels	3 ft 8 in.

Governess Cart *Plate 8*

This illustration shows a small type of cart or car which took its name from the fact that it was ideal for use by the governess of a household.

The governess cart was a form of tub cart with low hung body and rear entrance where the occupants were safely transported behind a quiet pony. The driver and passengers all sat on side seats facing inwards as in the wagonette, and because it was often used to take the children for a trip it was slung low between the wheels but with high sides to prevent youngsters falling out or putting their hands in the wheels.

Bodies were panelled or railed or basket work construction or a mixture to suit the purchaser. To provide a low floor a cranked axle was used as in the float, and full elliptic springs ensured a smooth ride.

This style of vehicle became popular around 1900 and found great use by country houses where the children could be despatched for the day under the care of the governess and a quiet pony or donkey leaving the coachman and groom free to attend to the master's carriage.

Prairie Schooner *Plate 9*

During the great migration of settlers across the American continent in the mid nineteenth century, all sorts of vehicles were pressed into use to carry the family and its belongings to the promised land. Some travellers used the farm wagons that they had prior to setting off on their long trek while others had to get one specially for the journey. Whatever type of vehicle was used it was only those that were strongly constructed that could hope to survive the transcontinental journey of some 2,000 miles spread over two, three or even four months of mobile hardship.

The style of vehicle which became known as the prairie schooner because of its white canvas cover standing out in the wilderness like a sail in the ocean, was a four-wheeled wagon with a couple of oxen or mules up front. The body consisted of an open box about 12 ft long and 4 ft wide with sides about 2 or 2½ ft high. Attached to the outside of the body were five or six curved top bows or hoop sticks of hickory supporting a strong canvas or perhaps two cotton sheets. At front and rear the cover was extended beyond the ends of the body by sloping the bows and some measure of end protection was afforded by pulling the cover tight by drawstrings. Alternatively in fine weather the strings could be undone and the cover thrown back for ventilation.

Wheels of about 4 ft and 5 ft diameter were used to maintain reasonable ground clearance to rocks and streams and these were mounted on hardwood axle beds. Above each axle and secured to it by long bolts was a bolster which supported the wagon body or bed. These bolsters were extended part way up the body sides for added security.

A long centre reach or perch connected the front and rear axles; bolted to this were the hounds, two of which braced the rear axle and another two maintained rigidity to front axle and wagon tongue or draught pole. A box was usually provided at the front of the wagon to hold a few tools for repairs, and a canvas bucket was slung beneath the vehicle with brush and grease for lubrication. A seat was fixed either on the front of the wagon or just within the cover and tied to the outside there might be a water barrel, plough, shovel, pick and cooking pots.

Under the cover was just about everything the emigrants could take on their journey, although no doubt a lot of items were shed on the way be they to lighten the load or to barter for supplies.

Oil and Colourman's *Wagon* *Plate 10*

This illustration shows a style of vehicle which was built in 1906 in Melbourne, Australia, for a firm of oil and colourmen or what today one would call builders merchants handling all forms of building materials, paint and glass.

The users of the vehicle specified that it should have a

double purpose being equally suitable for carrying sheet glass as well as the general merchandise of their trade.

When used as a normal light wagon it had a 7-inch sided body which measured 8 ft 3 in. long and 4 ft 6 in. wide with a close boarded floor. In this guise it was eminently suitable for the sacks, jars, coils, bundles, boxes, bags, barrels and other collections of various materials stocked.

When it was necessary to carry large sheets of glass such as were needed for shop fronts then the vehicle underwent a change of appearance. First the wide seat was lifted off the front of the body, the four vertical tongues being withdrawn from the metal staples on the inside of the body sides. Next a large slat-bottom rack or platform was lowered on to the top of the body being secured by four vertical tongues engaging in metal staples on the inside of the body. This rack was considerably larger than the original body measuring 9 ft 9 in. long by 6 ft 6 in. wide. A single light seat was then dropped into two metal staples at the front of the body so the change was complete.

When engaged in glass-carrying a blanket was laid over the slatted floor and the sheets of glass laid on top with blankets between each. Finally a light mattress was placed on top and the whole roped down for security.

The specification for this type of wagon gave the length between axles as 5 ft 9 in. with the front wheels 2 ft 10 in. and the rear 3 ft 8 in. high. Both front and rear springs were 3 ft between centres and both sets of wheels were 5 ft 7 in. out to out.

Body framing was of $3\frac{3}{4}$ in. × $1\frac{1}{2}$ in. with $\frac{7}{8}$ in. side panels, floor was 8 in. × $\frac{7}{8}$ in. boards, and the slatted top section was of $2\frac{1}{4}$ in. × 2 in. framing with $2\frac{3}{4}$ in. × $\frac{1}{2}$ in. slats on top.

With demand for even larger sheets of glass to be transported a more specialised type of vehicle evolved. If the glass was in protective crates then these were carried on edge in a high sided wagon. In order to keep overall heights as low as possible, wagons with dropped axles or very small wheels were designed which produced a low floor line. When sheets of glass were carried singly or in a variety of large sizes then a special body was constructed with an inclined gantry in the centre against which the glass was stood on edge.

Camel Top Van *Plate 11*

The illustration shows a single horse van of about 25 cwt capacity having the arched roof at the front from which it gets its title.

This style of van was very popular with bakers, confectioners, pastrycooks, grocers and the like because it not only gave the van a pleasant curving line at the front end but it was functional by virtue of the increased headroom for ease of entry and egress.

A typical specification for a van of this type gives overall dimensions of the body as 9 ft long, 4 ft 8 in. high and 4 ft wide. It was carried on elliptic springs and 2 ft 10 in. high wheels on the full fifth wheel forecarriage while the rear axle was suspended on half elliptic springs and carried 4 ft 3 in. wheels.

The body bottom framing was carried out in oak 3 in. × 1¾ in. with the ¾ in. spruce floor boards rabbeted into it. The remainder of the body was framed in ash with panels of mahogany although in later designs panels of sheet metal or metal faced birch plywood were used. The roof was made of ¾ in. boards tongued and grooved, covered with moleskin and well painted.

The rear of the body was covered with a pair of hinged doors 3 ft 3 in. high and above them a wide Venetian was provided for ventilation but suitably screened on the inside with fine gauze to keep out the dust. At the front of the body behind the driver's seat there was a sliding door to gain access to the load. For bakers' use metal angle was screwed along both sides of the body to provide slides for trays.

Logging Truck *Plate 12*

Among the longest and the most sturdily built vehicles were the timber carriages and pipe carriers usually constructed with two-wheeled bolsters connected by a long backbone frame or pole.

One of the heaviest types of construction is the eight-wheeled logging truck shown in our illustration. This type of vehicle was for loads up to 10 tons and much of its time would be spent deep in the forests where it was used to haul out the massive logs or butts for transport to river or mill. It is built up of two similar carriages or gears each being made with four massive wheels 3 ft in diameter and 6 in. wide. The framing is made from oak, ash or hickory and well plated and a full fifth wheel is fitted to each bolster. All axles are connected by side chains to keep them more or less in line in cases of emergency. With the load in position a certain amount of flexibility is given to the vehicle by means of the two fifth wheels and the coupling between the two sets of gears.

Not all timber carriages were built on such heavy lines, they being built for various capacities right down to a light vehicle for carrying sawn lengths on hard roads. Between the two extremes came a wide variety of load carriers under various titles and sizes.

The majority of vehicles were four wheeled and built on the principle of two bolsters for securing the load carried on two pairs of wheels and connected by a long pole or perch. The front pair of wheels turned under a fifth wheel while the rear pair were rigidly attached to the bolster. The pole was permanently fixed to the forecarriage but was made to slide through a hole provided in the rear carriage so as to make the length between the bolsters variable to suit the load. In some parts of the world just the two carriages were taken into the forest where a suitable tree would be used to form the pole. Security of the pole in the carriage would be by metal spikes, wire rope or chains.

Another style of vehicle was a two-wheel drag which had very large wheels and was positioned over the log lying on the ground. A wire rope or chain was passed under the log and secured to the vehicle. By means of a windlass the rope was tightened and one end of the tree lifted off the ground. By this means the log could be dragged out of the forest. This system of lifting the log was also used in some designs of four-wheel vehicles for both timber haulage and the transport of long, large diameter pipes.

The timber carriages of the world went under different names with the terms carriage, vehicle, wagon, van, drag, trolley or lorry being used in Britain. America seemed to prefer timber or lumber truck, wagon, buggy, log truck or drag wagon while in Australia the term jinker, wagon and truck appear to be preferred.

Although the timber carriage underwent considerable punishment through its life, because of its heavy construction many of them survived the horse era and continued to give useful service behind steam tractors and petrol lorries.

Gooseneck Truck *Plate 13*

As mentioned elsewhere the horse-drawn vehicle came in a myriad of shapes and sizes to suit the particular job to be done, and although many different types are illustrated in these pages, there are far, far more.

A glance through the pages of the trade journals of the period or a nineteenth century coachbuilder's catalogue reveals an unbelievable array of vehicles to suit all manner of trades and almost every pocket.

There were special cradles for carrying reels of cable, low

loading trucks for carrying heavy loads, special low trucks for carrying boilers, very high sided trucks for theatrical scenery, iron carts for manure, road scrapers with rows of teeth, and vehicles with iron wheels for countries plagued with termites!

As the coachbuilding trade had originated from many local craftsmen it is not surprising that local names became attached to particular styles of vehicle, and so we find Cambridge carts, Scotch carts, Alderney dairy carts, Yarmouth fish carts and London vans. The export markets were handled by some of the larger producers and without exception they had special Colonial models aimed at the developing countries and colonies.

With the truck illustrated it is the shape of the body which gives rise to its title – gooseneck truck, again a name which is perpetuated in modern low loading truck trailers. The feature of this design is the way in which the load carrying portion of the vehicle is brought down to a low height by means of the drop frame and then supported on a cranked axle. This permits the use of full-size wheels at the rear. The forecarriage could also use normal size wheels but the drop portion of the frame had to receive special strengthening or the whole vehicle would sag in the middle.

Wagonette Brake *Plate 14*

The small wagonette had its origin in 1842 when Lord Curzon had one constructed for his use and very soon the design was copied by others. It was a vehicle for many purposes being able to hold luggage or hampers in addition to four or six passengers as well as two on the box. These vehicles were driven to a pair and because of their utility were often finished in varnished wood.

Later in the nineteenth century larger vehicles were built which included some with folding hoods for passenger protection, and the very large ones which required three or four horses.

The larger variety were known as wagonette brakes being used for a variety of tasks including horse exercising, station work, picnics, shooting parties and even for the transport of forage. It made an ideal vehicle for a day at the races or a country picnic because in addition to carrying a reasonable party of people there was space for hampers and baskets down the middle of the floor or under the seats. On some designs a waterproof cover was provided being supported on metal standards which slotted into staples along the body sides, and on others the seat cushions were removable, the seats hinged up to the sides and a spacious vehicle for luggage or other goods provided. A livery stable often found use for a wagonette brake being handy for collecting forage and other stores as well as being a substantial vehicle for training carriage horses.

Emergency Wagon *Plate 15*

This illustration depicts what is termed an emergency wagon designed primarily for use by street car and trolley car systems. Although these transport systems often had service vehicles which were built on car chassis with rail wheels these were in the style of routine maintenance cars being quite heavy in construction and capable of carrying large and heavy pieces of equipment.

To be independent of the rail tracks and the overhead power system the horse-drawn wagons were important although lighter. They were able to overtake cars blocking the lines and travel along roads not covered by the routes of the system.

Designed primarily for time of emergency when overhead power lines came down or were damaged by trolley poles, or when the work of the regular fireman was hampered by the presence of trolley wires, the vehicle was kept in a state of readiness at the depot. Upon being summoned by the telegraph alarm the duty linesmen would attach the horses and surmount the front part of the wagon. The rear part of the body was open and used to carry various tools and parts that might be required for the particular emergency.

Basic dimensions of the vehicle are as follows:

Body length	9 ft 10 in.
,, width	4 ft 0 in.
,, height	1 ft 5 in.
Front wheels	3 ft 2 in.
Rear wheels	4 ft 4 in.
Wheelbase	6 ft 8 in.
Track (out to out)	5 ft 2 in.

Street Flusher *Plate 16*

One of the leading builders of municipal vehicles in the United States, The Tiffin Wagon Company of Tiffin, Ohio, was established in 1874 and achieved considerable success with their wide range. Products included two-wheel carts, tipping carts and garbage trucks, four-wheel dump wagons, heavy trucks, teamster gears, steel bucket garbage trucks, farm wagons and street sprinklers and flushers.

The illustration shows one of the later type of street flusher produced up to the mid-1920's which was still horse-drawn although a petrol engine was provided to power the flushing apparatus. Earlier models of street watering carts were termed sprinklers because originally only gravity was used to spray the dusty streets with water. Soon after the advent of the automobile, Tiffin could see the greater potential of a powered water feed to flush right across the street on each journey, so a car engine was installed at the rear to drive a two-stage centrifugal pump. This was the 700 gallon model with steel tank mounted on 34 in. and 52 in. wheels and employing a Continental 'N' model 4 cylinder 20 hp petrol engine for powering the pump. The engine was hand cranked from the rear and gravity fed from a 14 gallon tank and employed water from the main tank for cooling purposes. Unladen weight was 4,900 pounds.

Other vehicles in the range were of 300, 450, 600 and 650 gallon capacity metal tanks with either side of rear sprinklers and for areas with no problems of woodworm a wooden tank could be supplied!

Mail Cart *Plate 17*

The widely varying designs and styles of vehicle used for carrying the mails over the years is a subject which in itself could easily fill several volumes. Indeed in Britain there is the Post Office Vehicle Club which caters purely for students of postal transport, and the carriage of the mails from forked stick to rocket has already been adequately described.

In both Britain and America the vehicles used for mail carriages were usually had on hire from transport contractors, so absolving the postal authorities from the trials and tribulations of finding suitable vans and horses in every part of the country. With this system the vehicles came in a wide assortment of style and size varying from tiny pony traps at outlying areas through to large heavy vans drawn by speedy four-in-hand teams for long distance transport.

The illustration shows a typical small U.S. mail cart design of around the turn of the century. The original specification mentions that it was for collecting mail from large office buildings in New York City, but was unpopular with the drivers because there was no protection for them!

The body was 4 ft 10 in. long and 3 ft 0 in. wide and was mounted on 4 ft 3 in. wheels. Side springs were 3 ft 10 in. long and the body springs 3 ft 5 in. long.

Later styles featured enclosed bodies some with sliding doors, some vehicles had fitted shelves for mail sorting and storage while other designs used double skin sides with wood inner panels and metal outers. Some had locking doors for security while other designs merely used a curtain at the rear. Colour schemes varied widely too. In some vehicles the main body colour was red while in others it was blue, some had a mixture of red, white and blue while others were just one plain shade.

Lettering usually consisted of United States Mail or U.S. Mail with the U.S.M. cypher placed together with the contractor's name and a fleet number.

Dump Wagon *Plate 18*

The dump or dumping wagon grew out of the need for a vehicle which could move a sizeable load of earth, rock, sand or aggregate and dump it, perhaps while moving over rough ground, in a position required by the road builder without fear of capsizing the vehicle.

Early designs of tip carts were of the two wheel variety relying on balance and perhaps a bit of brute strength but particularly on skill and experience on the part of the driver. Later designs extended to four-wheel carts some using mechanical screw lifting gear, others using rollers, some gravity operated pivoting tipping and another a system of steel wire wound on to a drum. All these designs utilized the principal of rearward tipping which, if carried out on uneven ground could result in the vehicle being overturned by an unwary driver.

The bottom dumping wagon was an improvement because the discharging action took place between the wheels so giving maximum stability at all times. As the rate of discharge could be controlled from the driver's seat it was possible to spread the load over a given area. This feature was particularly attractive to railroad builders, road graders and farmers. As time went on some manufacturers made a special study of dumping wagon design and these were improvements and patents in respect of bottom door construction, door sealing, mechanical operation, axle design, wheel construction, attachment of draught gear, etc.

The illustration shows a 1907 design of dumping wagon produced by the 'largest vehicle manufacturers in the world' – the Studebaker Brothers Manufacturing Co. of South Bend, Indiana. In their design Studebaker claimed that they had the 'latest, strongest and best dump wagon on the market' with such features as exceptionally strong wheels to resist damage by rocks on site work, full fifth wheel for site stability, heavily plated undergear for strength, single chain operated dumping gear for simplicity and an arched rear axle to avoid dragging of dumped load. The body was of hardwood construction adequately plated for strength and the doors were lined with sheet steel as a guard against wear and to provide an overlapping seal as they shut. Four substantial hinges on each door kept them in line to prevent spillage, and the chain operated discharge gear was compensated for wear. The pole and draught equalizer were connected to the front axle to ensure direct draught by the horses.

Other designs of dump wagon were produced by the Michigan Wagon and Manufacturing Co. of Jackson, Mich.; Columbia Wagon Co., Columbia, Pa.; Watson Wagon Co. of Canasota, N.Y., and the Tiffin Wagon Co. of Tiffin, Ohio. The Troy Wagon Works Company of Troy, Ohio, boasted that their design of wagon would enable liquid concrete to be carried up to a mile without fear of spillage or setting en route, and the Symons design marketed by the Contractors' Supply and Equipment Co., of Chicago, Ill., had doors which opened fore and aft instead of sideways.

Barouche *Plate 19*

The barouche has been described as the principal of all open carriages being extremely graceful and equal to an open coach in line and appointment.

Construction was with a perch and C-springs for the carriage with the elegant open body suspended on leather braces. The driving seat was framed up to the body and was wide enough to accommodate both driver and footman, there being no rear platform for servants. It is interesting to read what W. Bridges Adams had to say in 1837 about this arrangement; I quote '. . . the hinder part being unprovided with a standard, which would be useless, as when the head is down there is little convenience for the servant's holders, and he would, moreover, be unpleasantly placed, looking down on the sitters within and listening to all the conversation.'

So that was the viewpoint in 1837.

The barouche was essentially a town vehicle and primarily for summer use, there being no facilities for storage or luggage on the vehicle and only a folding hood to protect passengers' heads and a folding cover to keep the rain off their legs. Even these limited facilities were for the forward facing passengers, the barouche being provided with two seats and those sitting behind the driver had to fend for themselves or squeeze into the rear seat.

Other styles of body were produced including one with an upholstered rear seat for servants which would probably have dismayed Mr Adams! In another style both C-springs and elliptic springs were used – an eight-spring barouche, and on another there was no seat for the driver this style evidently being postillion driven.

Normally a pair of horses were used for the barouche but because of its suitability for procession work it frequently appeared with four or even six horses and on these occasions was in the hands of a postillion.

Pick up a book on carriages and read the story of its beginning; chances are it will say it was introduced from Paris by the Prince of Wales in 1869, or 1870, or 1860 or 1850. Read another book and it will say the design was evolved from the pony phaeton of George IV in 1824. Another tells us it was evolved from the cab phaeton produced in France as the Milord, and yet another report has it that it came from the drawing board of J. C. Cooper the London coachbuilder.

These explanations are only mentioned to show how difficult it is to put precise dates and designers to some types. Many coachbuilders saw a design and liked the general lines so decided to build one, then feeling it needed a bit of personality or modification for some particular use or client set about varying the original design. So hardly any two carriages were exactly alike.

Getting back to the Victoria we find general agreement in that whatever its lineage, originator or parentage it was a light open carriage with low entrance, no doors, a folding hood, splash guards over the wheels, and was coachman driven for one or two horses. Variations came in the way of a rearward folding seat, a fixed double rearward facing seat, very low doors, C-springs and perches, Morgan C-spring and leather braces, panelled boot, angular body style, etc.

Whatever variety of Victoria was fashionable at that particular moment it remained a popular carriage right through the reign of the Queen. Essentially a fine weather vehicle the folding hood was useful during a shower but the design was so 'open' that it was a perfect foil for the fine ladies dresses of the period. The low step and entrance made entry simple and once seated the occupants had a good view of their surroundings and passersby of them.

Our illustration shows the North American version of this popular European carriage.

Phaeton *Plate 21*

This illustration shows an American design for a four-passenger phaeton mounted on rubber tyres. This is a late design of vehicle from the period just before the First World War when bodywork for automobiles was fast becoming more profitable, and signs of this appeared in horse-drawn vehicles such as automobile seats, plywood bodies, man-made timber panels, metal-faced plywood sheets, torsion springs and metal panels.

In this design the seat is very automobile looking but was built up of boards with solid poplar corner pillars the whole being rounded off and mouldings used to cover the joints.

The rear seat is covered with a $\frac{5}{16}$ in. panel recessed into the corner pillars and the joints covered by mouldings. The panels are of wood on the inside and metal outside.

The designers of the period were trying to copy automobile bodies with curved metal panels, and whereas earlier horse-drawn bodywork had been rather square in appearance or at the most curved in one plane the modern trend was to produce three dimensional curved surfaces.

In the style of the vehicle illustrated the specification gave the following details:

Overall length	9 ft 6 in.
,, dash to rear of body	6 ft 9 in.
,, width of body	6 ft 9 in.
,, height	5 ft 2 in.
Height of wheels with rubber tyres 36 in. and 45 in.	

Surrey *Plate 22*

This illustration shows the style of American vehicle which received a lot of recognition in later years because of the popular song about the fringed top variety. In an American summer there was probably nothing nicer than a ride in an elegant Surrey, with its high seats giving a good view, the picturesque fringed top warding off the hot sun, the open sides catching the breeze and the gentle whirring of the wheels beneath those graceful sweeping fenders.

Like most American pleasure vehicles the wheels of the Surrey were near equirotal. It was usually built on the basis of a light centre spine or perch which forked at its rear end, suspension was by transverse elliptic springs attached to the extreme front and rear of the body. It was either a brother or cousin of the buggy, but whatever its relationship it was certainly more elegant and indeed expensive. The cheapest vehicle was undoubtedly the buckboard which consisted of a long board, a seat, two axles, four wheels and little else. The buggy and the runabout came next probably followed by some of the wagons but it is difficult to categorize all the variations and looking through old designs one man's buggy was another man's wagon if you know what I mean. Whatever title these little vehicles went under it was generally accepted that if you acquired a Surrey you had arrived at a certain station that was the envy of a lot of your friends!

Depot Wagon *Plate 23*

An extremely popular vehicle in the United States was the depot wagon which found great use as both passenger and load carrier. As with almost every other kind of vehicle the term was applied to a variety of styles having various features. In all cases they were four-wheeled and had a rigid roof supported on pillars, but from there on they varied widely.

Some designs were almost identical to the Rockaway (Plate 24) with no rear door and they came in either reach undergear or suspended on elliptic springs. Some had glass frames in the side doors and rear quarters and perhaps the front as well. In some instances these glasses were made to drop. Other designs for hot climates just had roll up side curtains while others had screen sides to keep out flies.

Probably the type which typifies the style most accurately is that which had glasses in the two hinged side doors and the front panel and open rear quarters and a drop tailboard at the rear for easy stowage of goods or baggage.

Rockaway *Plate 24*

The poor man's coach in North America was the rockaway, being a somewhat similar design to the depot wagon but unlike that vehicle it was meant purely for passengers' use.

Because of vagaries in the annual climate it was usually constructed as an enclosed vehicle but had the glass sashes in the front and doors able to drop or be removed entirely in hot weather. Some users liked to have mesh screens to keep out the flies while others had rolled up side curtains. Doors could be made panelled up to the elbow line while some preferred them very low as in the illustration.

The style of vehicle shown is a late design from the period before the First World War.

Overall length	9 ft 9 in.
,, width of body	3 ft 8 in.
,, height	7 ft 3 in.
Length, dash to rear of body	7 ft 0 in.
Wheels with rubber tyres	34 in. and 44 in.
Front springs	35 in. long.
Rear springs	36 in. long.

Hansom Cab *Plate 25*

One of the most famous of horse-drawn vehicles must be that forerunner of the modern taxi cab – the Hansom cab.

Named after the designer of the original style of 'cab', which was of the single horse variety with large wheels, a low centre of gravity and with the driver positioned high up, the type was improved upon by others culminating in the design by John Chapman which is still termed a Hansom.

Joseph Aloysius Hansom was an architect who had studied the then current styles of vehicles used for hire as Hackney cabs and in 1834 decided that something better was needed. His resultant design was for a large square vehicle carried by a pair of 7 ft 6 in. diameter wheels which had their short stub axles positioned in about the centre of the body so that passengers might easily enter by way of the nearside front door. By virtue of the size and mounting of the wheels it also rendered the vehicle extremely stable. The driver was positioned up aloft at the front of the body which incidentally had louvre type ventilators at the front.

The story has it that this vehicle was not a complete success in its original guise and was altered by fitting small diameter wheels, removing the front louvres and positioning the driver actually on the front of the roof.

Soon after this John Chapman of the Safety Cabriolet and Two-Wheel Carriage Company looked at Hansom's designs and set about producing his own cab. In his design the wheels were carried on a deeply cranked axle which passed right under the body of the cab, windows were provided in the sides and a pair of padded half doors at the front provided protection for the passengers. The driver was positioned at the rear of the body high enough to be able to see the horse's head and most of the road around his cab. The Chapman design was patented in 1836.

For many years the Hansom was a very popular vehicle and the design was copied by many coachbuilders and cab proprietors. No doubt because of its small size, lightness cheapness and general convenience many Hansoms were acquired by private individuals and used in preference to larger carriages when the load was small and appearance of no consequence.

State Landau *Plate 26*

One of the most graceful styles of open carriage ever designed, the British State landau as it is known in official terminology is more often called a canoe landau by the experts because of the graceful curve of the bottom.

This type of carriage is said to have had its origins in Germany at the town of Landau in about 1757 [G. A. Thrupp] and in original form was a coach suspended on whip springs and leather braces above a straight perch. The distinguishing feature of the design which ensured its subsequent success and widespread adoption in other parts of Europe, the United States and Australasia was the way in which the head could be folded down in two sections, to the front and rear, so that if the window sash was dropped into the door panel and both heads pushed back the enclosed coach was transformed into an open carriage.

In later designs the perch was curved down and the floor brought nearer the ground; C-springs were substituted for the almost upright whip springs; the use of elliptic springs and the dispensing of the perch and a drop well in the centre made entry and exit much simpler. Probably the most important improvement was the experimental work done in getting the twin hoods to lie flat so as to render them almost unnoticeable when open.

As with many vehicles names have become attached to various designs because of links forged with sales to titled customers. The square landau is sometimes referred to as the Shelbourne and the curved bottom or canoe style as the Sefton, both being named after English earls.

The landau illustrated is of a type which can be seen in the Royal Mews at Buckingham Palace in London where it is kept for use in State processions or on other formal occasions.

Mail Coach *Plate 27*

Another of the type of vehicles about which much has been written is the mail coach.

The British mail coach originated in 1784 when John Palmer MP who was proprietor of a theatre in Bath and who had need to regularly use the current postal system of post-boys on horseback, asked Parliament to let him use his coach for mail carrying. He had become so angry with the slow and unreliable service that he set about using his private carriage for carrying the post. He succeeded in persuading HM Government that he could provide a better service and with the Bath to London service as the first he quickly set about proving his words. Not long after he was asked to extend his services to other major centres.

In the next two years the service was extended to such towns as Dover, Portsmouth, Exeter, Leeds, Liverpool, Manchester and Birmingham the contractors supplying the coaches using ordinary stage coaches modified in accordance with the wishes of the Post Office.

Although the system was a good one for the Post Office and was an improvement on the service previously encountered, it did play havoc with the coaches and steps were taken to seek improvements in the design and construction of the vehicles in order to render them less liable to failure. Various designs were inspected and one by John Besant adopted, this design including that of the improved 'mail axle' which type remained in use up to the end of the coaching era with the coming of the railways.

The style of vehicle shown in our illustration is the final arrangement with the fore and hind boots framed into the body and both forecarriage and hind axle carried on a set of four springs arranged in the form of a rectangle and called the 'telegraph spring'. The early mail coaches were blue and orange with the black and maroon livery appearing later and lasting until the end in 1842.

Australian Mail Coach *Plate 28*

Illustrated in this plate is one of the stage coaches operated by the famed Cobb & Co. of Australia an operation which commenced in 1854 and continued for 70 years.

Freeman Cobb was working for Adams & Co., a firm of express agents in San Francisco: together with three others he went to Melbourne in 1853 to set up an Australian branch with financial backing from G. F. Train of tramway fame. There were already some coaches operating in Australia but these were built in England and Cobb wanted to use the American Concord coaches that he thought would better stand the Australian 'roads'. Accordingly coaches and harness were sent from America and the first coach service commenced from Melbourne to the goldfields at Forest Creek a distance of some 84 miles. This service had been started with wagons while awaiting the arrival of coaches.

The original coaches were genuine Concord Jack coaches with the deeply curved bottom to the body suspended on thick leather thoroughbraces slung from iron pillars. They had a glass sash in the door and roll up leather blinds to the quarters. At the rear was a wedge shaped boot with stout canvas cover for luggage and the roof was railed round for further storage. Colours were red body, yellow gear, crimson plush seats and fancy gold scrollwork and flower designs on the panels.

In later years as the company expanded a coach factory was started at Charleville, and with years of coach operation behind them a 'Cobb & Co.' design of coach developed which embodied features found in the local wagons based on German designs. The imported American vehicles were too light for the treatment they received in Queensland, and Cobb & Co. subsequently ordered replacements from Stevenson & Elliot of Melbourne based on the Concord wagon design but with certain modifications. The locally built vehicles were squarer than the imported ones and a lot less ornate in interior comfort.

Dairy Float *Plate 29*

So far as business vehicles go, one of the most attractive and popular with the public attending shows is the dairy or milk float. Several of these smart little vehicles have been restored to their former glory and whenever they appear at shows are always sure to be of a warm reception.

The basic design is for a two-wheeled float or cart with a low floor line usually incorporating a cranked axle. The driver either stands or sits at the rear of the vehicle by the entrance and the inside is fitted with churn racks, iron loops for a hand can and a crate for small cans.

Variations on the basic theme were carried out by many wheelwrights and coachbuilders to suit the particular whim or fancy of the user. One design might call for the float to have straight side panels while another liked the upper part of the body to project slightly. Some people liked the float to have nicely curved splashers covering the top and rear part of the wheels and others liked a small curved splash guard at the top quarter of the wheel. Most liked to have a panel large enough to prominently display their name somewhere and some adorned their floats with pictures of cows grazing in grassy fields or attached a pair of horns or a cow's head to the front of the float! Above all the float had to give the appearance of cleanliness because before the advent of milk in glass bottles it was all dispensed by a measuring can from the churn into your own jug. So the painting and finishing of the float was as important as its construction and plenty of highly polished brass rails and fittings were used to achieve a bright finish. White, cream, light blue and brown were the favourite colours with adequate lining to show off the lines.

Typical specifications of the day called for a cream body with brown lining, gold on edges of display boards; wheels and springs brown with royal green lines; all metalwork in brown. Another specified that the body was in pale blue with framing in white, all gold lined with shafts and wheels in dark blue lined in white. Nameboard was with white ground and gold letters, edged with brass.

Even as late as the mid-1920's British dairy farmers emigrating to Australia were amazed to find that the local vehicles had a high set body which made loading and unloading difficult so Australian coachbuilders were prevailed upon to build floats of the 'English type'.

Most of the dairy floats were light vehicles designed for ponies or horses of 14–15 hands. The loads carried were not large and in sparsely populated areas there might be a fair distance between customers. As the dairies gradually became larger combines and the milk was sold in glass bottles carried in teak crates, so loads became heavier and the little milk float was ousted in favour of larger, four-wheel covered vans capable of greater loads in the denser areas.

Butcher's Cart *Plate 30*

Said by some to be the fastest thing on two wheels the butcher's cart shown in this plate vied with that of the dairy float for being the smartest trade turnout of the day. The stories of their high speed and reckless driving emanate from the fact that they were often driven by the butcher's boy, while the older staff were busy cutting and serving in the shop. One can easily imagine the butcher's boy resplendent in striped apron and straw hat sitting on top of the equally smart little cart with a spirited cob between the shafts with only the white ribbon of the road before him. No wonder it was his wont to show a turn of speed as he went upon his deliveries, stopping his smart turnout at the 'tradesmen's entrance', chatting to the kitchen maids, and warding off the hungry dogs and cats of the neighbourhood!

Butchers' or purveyors' carts were mostly of the two wheel variety for delivery work, with the large four wheeled types reserved for wholesale deliveries or market work. The body was roughly rectangular with a compassed top surrounded by a rail for the baskets used in this trade. The body interior would be either one complete space or it may have removable sliding shelves carried on side angle pieces or some buyers preferred hooks for hanging joints etc. Access to the body was usually by means of a single or pair of doors at the rear although some of the larger carts had an opening top which was easier for loading carcasses.

For ventilation purposes Venetian slats were provided on both sides and perhaps at the rear but these would be covered with perforated zinc on the inside to prevent entry of flies.

Construction of the cart would probably be with bent ash shafts, body framing of oak $1\frac{3}{4}$ in. thick with $3\frac{3}{4}$ in. bottom sides, body sides of $1\frac{3}{16}$ in. ash and a floor of $\frac{3}{4}$ in. elm boards. The seat board would be 1 in. thick birch while the footboard was elm of the same thickness. The compassed top would be of $\frac{5}{16}$ in. pine boards covered with moleskin or canvas and 'sleeked' with a mixture of gold size and keg lead for waterproofing.

Fish Delivery Van *Plate 31*

The illustration shows a typical delivery van produced at the zenith of horse vehicle production in the period immediately preceding the First World War. This was the era of specialization in the field of bodybuilding with various firms finding it advantageous to go in for series production of a handful of hopefully popular designs rather than build a myriad of slightly differing types in order to satisfy the fancy of a multitude of users.

This trend of specialization went even further than just complete vehicles. Some firms decided to specialize in wheels, axles, undergear, bodies, brake systems or just in municipal bodies or dump bodies. The degree of specialization was of help to other bodybuilders as well as to actual users of vehicles. One instance of this was the production of wheels which was a tedious business when built singly as was the case with small local bodybuilders. With the era of specialization they were able to buy ready-made wheels in a wide variety of sizes to suit all kinds of vehicles they might be called upon to build. This left them free to concentrate on the production of specialized or custom built bodywork outside the scope of the volume producers and so the era of factory built bodies brought about changes in different aspects of the business.

Some of the firms specializing in delivery vans such as that illustrated were Finnesey & Kobler of Philadelphia; Maryland Wagon Works of Baltimore; Richards & M'Laughlin Wagon Co., Philadelphia; Schurmeier Wagon Co., Minneapolis; Frank Schanz of Philadelphia and the RechMarbeker Company of Philadelphia.

There was much competition between builders to produce something 'different' and so gain a slight edge on their contemporaries. Even a simple design might be enhanced by sweeping lines to exaggerate the curved top; a side window might be of extra size or of bevelled glass, extremely fancy lamps might be fitted or an extravagant use of brass employed to give the vehicle a showy appearance.

The van illustrated was built for a payload of between 1,000 to 1,500 lbs and has dimensions of:

Overall length	8 ft 10 in.
,, height	8 ft 3 in.
,, width	6 ft 2 in.
Body length	8 ft 7 in.
,, height	4 ft 9 in.
,, width	5 ft 0 in.
Track (out to out)	5 ft 2 in.

The paint job is worthy of note being typical of the high standard of work carried out by the painters, artists and sign-writers of the period.

This was the time when many business vehicles were beautifully turned out with pictures and lettering of a high standard. Businessmen of the day thought that a well turned out vehicle was a credit to its owner and should be recognized as such taking great pains to create an impression of well-being for their company and quality for their merchandise. A far cry from many vehicles of today which do little to enhance their owners' reputations or to reassure the customer of the cleanliness of the goods therein. A point of view borne out by a public house tenant who, upon seeing a tanker outside his house thought it had come to clean out the drains. To his dismay it was delivering his beer!

Coal Van *Plate 32*

In the dark foggy days that London was subjected to before the creation of smokeless fuel and the Clean Air Act, there was a great coal trade busy feeding the thousands of home fires.

The coal came into London by coal fired steam trains from the coalfields of Yorkshire, Nottinghamshire and South Wales and the long lines of wagons were gradually broken down and shunted hither and thither until finally clanking to a standstill at the local coal depot. In the larger depots the wagons were variously handled by engine, capstan, horse or gravity and eventually deprived of their contents by being tipped into large overhead hoppers whence the coal ran down to be weighed and measured into sacks for loading on to the delivery vehicle. In the smaller depots the coal had to be shovelled by hand out of the railway wagons into the sacks.

In various parts of Britain coal delivery vehicles went under different names. There were vans, lorries, lurries, carts and trolleys some being just a plain flat body with headboard to stabilize the first row of sacks. Another type had a high solid headboard which gave plenty of room for the name of the merchant and it was fitted with a very high metal rail running down the centre of the vehicle to give stability to the load. This centre rail often carried a top board about 8 in. deep which could be used to advertize the merchant's name.

Yet another style, with compassed front is shown in this illustration and this type was used to a large extent in the London area. The one distinct disadvantage of the type was that it had to be loaded and unloaded from the back so was not suitable for carrying a variety of coals because of the problems associated with sorting en route.

Coal vans of the type illustrated were made in various sizes to suit the requirements of the merchant being made with a pole for two or three horses or with one or two pairs of shafts.

A typical specification for a compassed front coal van:

Body length	8 ft 3 in.
Body width	4 ft 2 in.
Front wheels	3 ft 11 in.
Rear wheels	4 ft 7 in.
Front springs	2 ft 8 in.
Rear springs	3 ft 2 in.

Main body framing was in oak with deal floorboards and with birch side name panels. The compassed front panel was of sheet iron suitably finished with the merchant's name in vitreous enamel. Side upright standards were of $1\frac{1}{2}$ in. × $\frac{7}{16}$ in. iron with middle and top raves of $1\frac{1}{4}$ in. × $\frac{7}{16}$ in. Iron standards on compassed front were $\frac{3}{4}$ in. rod. An iron frame was positioned just below body at rear to take weighing scales; small detachable metal price plates being carried on either side and metal rubbing plates were rivetted to either side to prevent damage to sacks when front wheels were locked over.

Bulk Gas Van *Plate 33*

During the last quarter of the nineteenth century the horse-drawn vehicle was accelerating to almost the ultimate in its design, construction and execution. True the factory system was gaining a hold on the industry and to some this sounded the death knell of craftsmanship, but to others less purist in their outlook it was only a logical step in a competitive world where the market demanded something cheaper and better all the time.

Since that period when the mechanical vehicle began to oust the horse from its place on the road there has been an almost complete reversal in something that at first sight has nothing to do with the subject of this bulk-packaging. However, if we take a closer look at this particular subject we find that it is almost inseparable from a study of vehicles because almost all transportable items have to be packed or packaged in some way.

In our horse-drawn days there were few vehicles built to carry finished or part finished goods in bulk. True there were carts carrying farm produce, coal, roadstone etc. in an unpacked condition but these are really basic raw materials. It is only recently that we have had bulk tankers carrying liquids, powders and gases such as beer, milk, eggs, flour, sugar, petrol, oxygen and liquefied petroleum gas.

Somewhat of a paradox actually prevails when we find that

some other items which one used to be able to buy loose now come in small prepacked quantities. In our old horse-drawn days whereas shops sold biscuits loose from large tins, nowadays they come in sealed plastic packets. The old corn chandler sold his rice and beans out of a sack which stood on the floor but now they come in small cans or plastic bags. So the ever changing method, style and size of packaging has been reflected in changing types of vehicle bodywork carrying the goods.

It therefore comes as a bit of a surprise to find that as early as the 1860's one Parisian entrepreneur had constructed the vehicle illustrated for carrying gas in bulk. Evidently there was a demand for gas (of the coal extraction type) in the outer parts of the French capital which the pipe lines had failed to reach so this enterprising gentleman set about taking gas in bulk tanks to the customers.

The reference does not say if the vehicle was specially constructed or was an adaptation of an existing vehicle. If the original engraving is at all accurate in detail it would seem that the bodywork is of robust construction with standards curving under the body. Beneath the main floor is a kind of well section which appears to run the full length of the vehicle and in this well at the rear are the valves and connections for filling the cylinders at the gas producing plant and for transferring the gas to the customers' storage tanks at the point of sale. Just above the main filling valve is a manifold with connections to the nine storage cylinders and a solitary pressure gauge. Judging by the small portholes along the sides of the body the vehicle could have started life as a prison van.

Motor Car Lorry *Plate 34*

Once a fine carriage had been built it had to be delivered to the user, and if this was close to the coachbuilders all that was necessary was to harness up the necessary horses and drive it away. With the gradual decline in the number of 'local' coachbuilders the area of delivery increased with the result that delivery might take more than one day or the carriage might receive damage en route.

To alleviate some of the problems carriages were often conveyed by railway being end loaded at stations on to what were called 'carriage trucks'. For the large coach builders who were railway connected this was simple but if the railway station was a long way off the carriage may have to be driven to the station for loading or be loaded on to a horse-drawn carriage trolley for the initial journey.

With the advent of the horseless carriage and the building of some very expensive coachwork on similarly expensive car chassis, the job of transporting the completed motor car was handled by contractors using special 'motor car lorries' as shown in the illustration.

Whereas the earlier 'carriage trolley' could be made quite light because of the low weight of the modern carriage, the later style motor car lorry had to be more robust to withstand the weight of heavy ornate coachwork mounted on equally heavy motor powered chassis.

A typical specification for a motor car lorry of the type illustrated details the vehicle as being 14 ft 6 in. long, 5 ft 6 in. wide and 2 ft 8 in. loading height from the ground. A pair of loading ramps are supplied with the lorry and are fitted with stout iron hooks at the front end for hooking over the tailboard hinge pin and are tapered at the back end where they make contact with the ground. When not in use these ramps are slung beneath the body. A small windlass with length of wire rope is located on the headboard to assist with the loading of cars.

Construction of the lorry was relatively simple being a flat platform with small headboard and hinged tailboard. Body framing was of $2\frac{1}{2}$ in. oak with $\frac{7}{8}$ in. floorboards screwed on so that they could be easily replaced if necessary. The rear earbreadth was made particularly strong as it had to take a lot of weight when the car was being loaded; it was capped with a wide metal plate and finished off flush with the floorboards. Wheels were 2 ft high, with front springs 3 ft 3 in. long and rear 3 ft 6 in.

Garbage Truck *Plate 35*

The illustration is of an experimental type of improved garbage wagon introduced into use in Boston, Mass., early in 1910.

Earlier forms of garbage collection had involved vehicles into which the waste was tipped directly into the vehicle's body which in many cases was uncovered. The only covering had perhaps been a canvas cover thrown over the load and then only for the journey back to the tip or incinerator.

In the Boston design of wagon one of the major factors was that the openings in the containers carried on the vehicle were not much wider than the bin being emptied into it. This meant that little of the garbage remained uncovered and then for only short periods while a bin was being emptied into it. This feature reduced the chance of vast hordes of flies being able to settle on the rotting food, etc. and so lowered the chance of infection being carried back to the households.

Another attribute of the design was the fact that the greater part of the vehicle was made of metal and that the garbage receptacles were cylindrical, both points aiding the facility for adequate cleaning of the vehicle.

It should be noticed that the vehicle was built on the container principle which eased the handling of the loads of garbage at the depot when the full receptacles were hoisted from the wagon for emptying or for onward transmission to another site. A number of empty containers were then lowered into position and the garbage wagon could then go out on another round.

This design of vehicle was also an early attempt at making the job of collection easier on the men for the loading line was quite a reasonable height compared to some of the older styles where the bin had to be carried up a ladder for emptying. The Boston design also featured the idea of the loading aperture remaining closed until the operative had stepped on to a bar which was connected to the lid of the bin and opened by the application of his weight.

Hermaphrodite *Plate 36*

The Eastern counties of England tend to be both flat and fertile, so the farm wagons found in that area and in particular Essex were somewhat heavier than their counterparts elsewhere. With a lot of crops to harvest it was important that the vehicles stood up to heavy loads and more important were available at harvest time.

With most of the harvest being gathered in just about two months out of the year every available vehicle in the past was pressed into use and all the hay ladders were fitted to the wagons in order to provide maximum capacity.

Somewhere around 1800 some wide awake person saw the possibility of increasing the capacity of any available two-wheeled carts by temporarily converting them into four-wheeled wagons. Whether the idea was hit upon by lashing together two carts in tandem with some form of ladder between is one possibility but whatever its origin the hermaphrodite wagon was born somewhere in Essex during that period.

Basically the hermaphrodite was created out of an ordinary two wheel tumbrel, or Scotch cart or dung cart and a two-wheeled kind of forecarriage with shafts and a high bolster to support a foreladder.

The shafts of the cart were secured to the added forecarriage and a pole was secured to both the forecarriage and the underside of the cart or its axle. Then the top frame was positioned over the top of the cart body with its front end supported on the high bolster of the forecarriage. This top frame was used to carry the load although it did not cover completely the cart body so that this could still be used for the load. In some designs the top frame was made up of two parts: the foreladder which extended forward from the cart across the forecarriage bolster and projected over the horse's back; and from the back of the cart a second but smaller tail ladder sometimes extended being secured into staples on the rear of the cart body.

Peking Cart *Plate 37*

Mention China to the student of transport history and he immediately thinks of rickshaws, sedan chairs and Chinese wheelbarrows as being the media of that old civilisation. Other forms of transport did exist however including primitive ox carts with solid wheels and slat sides for farm and freight use, also long covered vehicles for the carriage of passengers plus a few fine carriages for the personal transport of the rich.

The chairs used varied greatly in style according to the rank or wealth of the occupant extending from very plain wooden seats on two plain poles to the most luxurious affairs covered in rich tapestries and ornamentation.

The Chinese wheelbarrow was that peculiar style with a large diameter wheel being positioned in the middle of the 'vehicle' and having space on either side for the carrying of goods or seating of passengers.

Rickshaws are something that have lasted right through the horse-drawn era and with its bicycle type wheels and a slim coolie up front it was capable of a good turn of speed for short distances.

The Peking cart illustrated was a vehicle peculiar to the area consisting of a small springless cart with a fabric cover and having the floor covered with quilts for the comfort of its passengers. A small horse, mule or donkey was used between the shafts and the driver either walked alongside or sat on the shafts.

Omnibus *Plate 38*

The name omnibus is said to have originated in about 1827 when M. Baudry a retired military officer who owned baths in the suburbs of the French town of Nantes, set up a regular service to the town centre using a coach named l'Omnibus.

His service was prosperous and he started services in other parts of France including of course, Paris. Other operators started up in competition and the Parisian coachbuilders produced vehicles in various forms.

One of the coachbuilders was an Englishman, George Shillibeer who, after serving in the Royal Navy, gained experience as a coachbuilder at Long Acre in London, and then set up business in Paris.

Prompted by the success of the new omnibuses in the French capital Shillibeer moved back to England and in 1829 put the first of his 'buses on the streets of London. The original L'Omnibus was like an enclosed wagonette with seats for eleven down each side, windows along the sides and at the front with a door at the rear. It was driven from a seat high up at the front of the body, carried on elliptic springs, and pulled by three horses.

The omnibus became popular and others followed Shillibeer's idea with routes starting in various parts of London, and after the passing of the Stage Coach Act in 1832, which authorised the picking up and setting down of passengers in the street, things expanded even further. Shillibeer's original style was not perpetuated however, because subsequent vehicles were smaller, had less seats and needed only two horses.

Unfortunately things did not go well for George Shillibeer and in 1836 he decided to quit the 'bus business. He sold his stock of twelve buses, twenty sets of pair harness, and the seventy-five horses in London and moved to Brighton where he invented a new combined hearse and mourners' carriage and continued as an undertaker until he died in 1866.

Meanwhile back in London the newly formed London General Omnibus Co. (established in Paris in 1855 as the Compagnie Générale des Omnibus de Londres), started acquiring many of the small independent operators by way of creating a giant amalgamation. In the following year it organized a competition for the best new design of omnibus upon which it could standardize its future fleet. The £100 prize went to R. F. Miller and it was upon his design that the new buses, which appeared in 1857 were based.

The formation of the double deck 'bus as we know it was gradual; extra passengers at first sitting alongside the driver; then the addition of a second seat crosswise on the roof enabled passengers to sit behind the driver; latterly the passengers being seated back to back across the roof. Designs with a raised centre portion of the roof, clerestory fashion, helped the roof seat idea and the general shape became known as the 'knifeboard' type. These 'Miller' design buses had a capacity of twenty-six passengers: twelve inside and fourteen on the roof.

As from 1881 London 'buses began to appear with a better seating arrangement on the roof or upper deck, this consisting of seats in pairs facing forwards. The rear access to the roof was much improved from the original rungs and steps to a proper, curving staircase. In modified form this arrangement continued to the end of horse bus operation in 1914 and the type acquired the name of 'garden seat' omnibus.

The illustration shows a London type garden seat omnibus of the 1890's working on a FAVORITE route between Stoke Newington and Victoria.

Private Omnibus *Plate 39*

The private omnibus was something of a cross between the open wagonette brake and the large covered public omnibus. It was an improvement on the wagonette brake by virtue of being a closed vehicle and a higher degree of comfort was possible for the occupants. Like the brake it had longitudinal seats and the entrance was through a full height door at the rear. The driving box was usually framed in to the main body of the vehicle and often the capacity was increased by an additional seat placed on the front of the roof with the driving boot forming a rest for the feet.

As this type of vehicle was often used for conveying a quantity of boxes, trunks, baskets and hampers when used for station work, race meetings, sports events or picnics the roof was railed round for the safe repository of such items this leaving the interior floor uncluttered.

For station work or a picnic a pair would probably be used with the vehicle but some houses might well desire the speed and power of a four-in-hand should a large party be going to a distant race meeting.

The vehicle became popular during the last quarter of the nineteenth century and of course many lasted till well into the motor age. Some large hotels situated some distance from the local station found them particularly useful and when not required for carrying passengers from the train the hotel bus could be hired by parties to enjoy tours of the locality. Where speed was not essential and the terrain not difficult some buses were driven to a single horse. There are still some hotels which favour the private horse-drawn omnibus for station work, and in some European resorts what better way to start a holiday than by stepping off the train into a beautiful example of nineteenth century coachbuilding complete with deep buttoned seats, silk blinds and a liveried driver!

Caravan *Plate 40*

The origin of the name caravan for a specific vehicle is not clear; it probably dates from the time when nomadic travellers on horseback took to using some kind of vehicle for carrying additional goods. The most common usage of the word was in connexion with a cart or wagon having a canvas top and this was probably the forerunner of the caravan as we know it today.

A similar vehicle was used by the pot dealers who hawked pottery around the country selling it at fairs and en route. They may have slept in the canvas covered cart or in a tent. A development of this arrangement was the 'accommodation' type used by some gypsies, consisting of a wooden tray about 6 ft × 4 ft × 9 in. fitted with wood hoops and covered with a canvas sheet. This was carried on a flat cart and could be lifted off and placed on the ground like a demountable frame tent.

The origin of the caravan or living van proper appears to be with a French traveller named Antoine Franconi who sometime during the early part of the nineteenth century built his 'voiture nomade' or traveller's vehicle. Some years later the idea seems to have crossed the Channel into England and the wooden living houses started to be used by travellers. After about 1850 they improved with the fitting of stoves and other internal fitments to aid the comfort of the users and different types evolved from the differing ideas of buyers and constructors throughout the country.

The early vehicles were often large and heavy requiring two

horses for draught but as the layout and requirements regarding fittings became more or less standard it was possible for a comfortable home to be produced within the length of about 12 to 14 feet and the weight kept down under a ton and nearer 15 cwt.

In the period up to the 1890's the styles settled down to about six basic types, but like the other horsed vehicles there were very many minor variations because of all vehicles these were the most personal. Historians generally agree that these types are the Reading wagon named after the town and depicted in the illustration; the Burton wagon originating at Burton-on-Trent; the ledge wagon because of its shape (upper part wider over wheels therefore forming a ledge); the bow-top or barrel-top wagon because of its sharply compassed roof shape; the open-lot because of the open front frame which forms a porch, and lastly the brush or fen so named after the brush dealers of the fens whose business decided the profusion of spindled racks and cases around the outside to hold the brushes.

Bridal Coach *Plate 41*

This plate reveals a design by a New York coachbuilder for a special coach for the use of the bride on the occasion of her wedding.

In their design of bridal coach the builders, James Cunningham, Son & Co., of Rochester, N.Y. set out to provide a fine and tasteful vehicle quietly befitting the occasion for the bride on 'her' day without it being too ostentatious and being likened to a circus band wagon. (See plate 67.)

In his design, J. Lawrence Hill of Cunningham's made frequent use of a heart shape, it appearing in the door carving, lamps, front and rear glasses and in the interior lining.

The coach undoubtedly had a light appearance and this was partly brought about by the ample use of glass at the front end so making the bride easily seen by her well wishers. The front lights, the front quarter lights and the door sashes were all made to drop and were further lightened in appearance by being framed in white mahogany.

The special electric lamps were silver plated as were the other metal fittings including a cluster of lights in the centre of the heart shaped, lace edged panel in the centre of the headlining. The interior lining of the coach was carried out in tufted satin for the head and upper quarters while the remainder was in cloth.

Diligence *Plate 42*

This illustration shows a style of vehicle which falls into the category of a diligence, stage coach or travelling coach.

The term diligence has found use as a long distance travelling coach both in England and on the European mainland.

An early description of such a vehicle is given by Roubo in his *L'Art du Menuisier-Carrossier* in which he describes the French diligences of 1760 as having large bodies with three small windows on each side and hung by leather braces on long perch carriages, with large hind wheels and low front wheels, without any driving box, and fitted with large baskets, back and front, for passengers or luggage. They were each drawn by five horses and driven by postillion on the off wheeler. One of these diligences was the first to be fitted with springs and ran between Paris and Lyons in five or six days according to the season.

An early illustration shows the diligence to be very similar to the ordinary coaches of the period but with the perch carried well back behind the hind axle and with a curving ironwork connecting the perch and the upright supports for the braces. The space created by this ironwork was used for carrying luggage which was covered by a large sheet attached to the back of the coach body.

Later designs of the diligence had the coach body but with a coupé body attached to the front looking like two vehicles stuck together. The driver was elevated to a position at the front of the roof with a folding hood for his protection. The roof was railed round for the stowage of luggage and to the rear of the roof were two seats char-a-banc fashion for the outside passengers. The whole was framed together to give the appearance of the later omnibus.

Some designs had hoop sticks over the roof for extra luggage or in fact any urgent freight which could bear the cost. Probably the best known vehicles of the diligence style were the Swiss postal coaches which carried the country's mails over some hazardous stretches of mountain road.

The Swiss diligence illustrated was the stagecoach of Europe.

Derby Cart *Plate 43*

Although horse-drawn vehicle and carriage-building generally has retained an air of quality and craftsmanship down to the present time, there are those that believe most of the quality of coachbuilding disappeared with the coming of the factory system. Whatever the truth of the matter there is no doubt that the factory system coupled to widespread advertising did result in some pretty impressive output figures from some of the larger establishments, and this high volume production coupled with a degree of specialization led to a lowering of prices.

However one French body designer at the turn of the century thought that the carriage trade had reached such a low state of affairs that everyone was chasing the ultimate in lightness and cheapness to the detriment of all that was dear to the coachbuilder.

He forthwith sat down and sketched out, or dare we say, designed his Derby cart as shown in the illustration. The specification called for the main body parts to be made out of $\frac{5}{8}$ in. or $\frac{3}{4}$ in. plain board but with metal plates bolted on the inside at front and rear to securely attached sides, ends and floor. The wings over the rear wheels were made from bent wood and that on the nearside was jointed so as to hinge the back rendering access to the rear seat easier.

The trimmer had only to make three cushions for the cart and these were to be trimmed in cloth for economy. The raised back was similarly treated and edged with a plain black metal band. The floor and the lower part of the door were covered with linoleum, the ironwork painted black and the woodwork given two coats of clear varnish.

Trailer Dustcart *Plate 44*

This illustration reveals a truly hybrid vehicle, because although a horse was employed to draw the dustcart, the trailer itself was in fact constructed to be towed by a motor vehicle.

The collection of refuse was carried out for very many years by horse traction and this state of affairs prevailed well into the motor vehicle era in many parts or the country. Because of the slow pace of the refuse vehicle as it toured the streets collecting all the dustbins and other waste, the work was well suited to the horse. A lot of the time the horse could be left to his own devices because a shout from one of the dustmen was all that was needed for him to plod on for a few more yards and then stop for the bins to be emptied. Another advantage was the way in which the horse could quickly be unhitched from the dustcart and attached to a completely different vehicle such as a road sprinkler, grass mower or tipper.

This was impossible with a rigid motor vehicle unless one went in for articulation or trailers or swop body systems.

However as time went on the desirability of motors became more apparent and the weight of arguments of being 'up-to-date' or uneconomic or non standard gradually ousted the horse.

Still the horse persisted in not being deposed completely and quite a few councils continued to use their horses in close collaboration with their motor fleet.

One of the failings of the horse on refuse collection was the slowness of getting back to the tip or incinerator with a full load because in many towns this may have been many miles from the point of collection. These longer journeys were best suited to the motor lorry so a compromise had to be made: horses for actual collection, motors for the journey to the tip.

The problem was tackled in two ways. The first was that the council bought a fleet of articulated dustcarts and specified the Scammell type of instantaneous coupling for speedy coupling and uncoupling of trailers. They also purchased the 'mechanical horse' (note the term) type of tractor unit for ease of manoeuvrability. The system was completed by the fabrication of special horse shafts complete with a pair of wheels and adaptor for the Scammell type of coupling. So now the horse could be used to take the refuse vehicles on their collection rounds while the 'mechanical horses' were kept busy shuttling back and forth to the tip with the vehicles full or emptied.

A somewhat similar system was designed by Walker Bros of Wigan, England, and in this case the horses pulled a specially constructed container on four wheels which when full was winched up on the back of a motor lorry for the journey to the tip. (See Plate 5 in *Lorries, Trucks and Vans since 1928*.)

Other cases of 'collaboration' in horse and motor transport were seen in the early days when many horse-drawn removal vans had the poles or shafts replaced by an iron towing attachment for use behind a steam tractor or motor lorry. During the experiments with the first designs of 'mechanical horses' by the London, Midland & Scottish Railway and Karrier

Motors some horse-drawn railway vans were adapted for use with the mechanical version of the equine variety of motive power. In more recent times of motor vehicle fuel shortage the horse has been called upon to provide the means of propulsion, and pictures taken in the Channel Islands during the last war showing cut down motor vehicles with a pair of shafts are surely enough to make a horse laugh!

Brewer's Dray *Plate 45*

In Britain the brewers have always been solid supporters of the various horse show events up and down the country continuing to provide smart turn outs right up to the present day. Even since the few years after the Second World War which really marked the end of commercial horse transport many of the British brewers continued to keep their horses. Firms such as Mann's, Whitbread's, Young's, Courage's, Thwaites' and others carried on with their horses in the 'heavy' classes which breeds included Shires, Clydesdales, Percherons and Suffolk Punch varieties. The brewer's dray was normally a pair horse turn out because of the weight of the beer in cask, but for the prompt delivery of bottled beers single horse vans with lighter breeds of horse were used.

It has been the heavier type of turn out which has remained probably because of the sheer magnificence of a fine pair of Shires or Percherons standing some 16 or 17 hands resplendent in their much polished harness. Added to which there is invariably a well painted and varnished dray sometimes complete with polished oak casks. Naturally this is their show standard and indeed some brewers have their horses purely for showing, but there are some who continue to use their horses for normal delivery work although in less fancy harness and with much more workaday drays.

Some of the drays in use are still those that have remained with the company since the nineteenth century while others have been updated by installing old trailer axles with pneumatic tyres. Others have been acquired from brewers that have gone out of business or just not continued with their horses. Some of the working drays can be seen delivering beer in the traditional wooden casks while others have bridged the transition in beer delivery by carrying shrink wrapped canned beer loaded on pallets by fork lift trucks!

In the illustration is shown a fine brewer's dray (or more accurately wagon) which used to attend shows in the late 1950's. Originally in the colours of J. W. Green of Luton, Bedfordshire, it was repainted in Flowers' name upon the formation of a new company when J. W. Green acquired Flowers of Stratford-upon-Avon. The same painting with an appropriate background is reproduced on the jacket of this book.

Florist's Van *Plate 46*

Over the years there have been many stories concerning the great hardship to which drivers were put in the pursuit of their jobs. In America, Australia, New Zealand and South Africa the overland stage coaches put up good performances against all kinds of problems. In England it was the mail coach drivers about which countless stories of personal ordeal were told. Generally speaking the driver of a horsed vehicle was a hardy character being subjected to the vagaries of the weather at all times and being afforded little protection from the elements.

It was not until the motor vehicle was firmly entrenched that better protection for drivers came about, and it was only when the horse-drawn vehicle was nearing the end of its career did we see protection in the shape of a windshield.

The vehicle shown in the illustration is a design for a florist's delivery wagon having plenty of glass all round including a windshield for the driver. The bottom frame of the body is of oak, the upright posts or standards are of ash, and the panels of poplar. The wheels are 34 in. and 37 in. high at front and back with a track of 5 ft. 2 in. out to out. The front springs are 3 ft 1 in. centres and the rears 3 ft 3 in.

The vehicle measures 11 ft long, 6 ft wide and 8 ft 8 in. overall height.

Wine Merchant's Van *Plate 47*

This illustration shows a small van operated by a Parisian wine merchant toward the end of the last century, and it is a typical example of the French 'camionette' of the period.

As with so many things, so in coachbuilding the French were acknowledged to hold the premier position with respect to producing a vehicle with balanced proportions and fine lines. Because of their natural talent for creating beautiful things coachbuilding was more an art than a trade to them and they were responsible for improving if not originating some fine designs of carriage.

The French vehicle builders tried to make their products pleasing to the eye as well as functional, and often a gentle curve here and a fancy bracket there, plus a well thought out paint scheme could make all the difference in the finished appearance. Sometimes the light vans had the lower panels painted several shades lighter than the vertical pillars and horizontal rails so as to accentuate the panelling, and this created a most pleasing effect. With flush sided vans the lower quarter might be painted in contrasting vertical stripes to relieve an otherwise sombre colour scheme. The lining out of panels was often done on the same basic colour as the panel, but several shades lighter, so the decoration was more refined than a scheme that used a boldly contrasting arrangement.

On the van illustrated a fancy curved roof board has been mounted which gives the little vehicle a subtle gay appearance putting it into a slightly better position when compared with a plain van having an ordinary bare curved roof line.

Prospector's Wagon *Plate 48*

This illustration shows a very light type of design for a prospector's wagon based on the near equirotal buggy or runabout style of construction.

The wheels were 40 in. and 44 in. high with a wheelbase of 60 in. and an overall length over the wheels of 102 in.

Because of the terrain across which the vehicle might have been driven it was well sprung having a torsion spring and a transverse half elliptic at the front while the rear axle was hung on two torsion springs and a full elliptic spring. The designer set out to provide for a normal load of about 400 to 500 lbs but by means of his springing allowed for an overload up to a further 300 lbs. In addition to the six springs of the vehicle suspension the intrepid prospector had his personal comfort further improved by means of the amply sprung seat, while the other end of his person was protected from sun and rain by a folding four bow top.

For carrying his tools, equipment, supplies and provisions the rear of the body had a 5 in. board round it plus a single detachable rail. A second seat could be fitted to the freight carrying part of the body secured by four staples screwed to the inside of the body sideboards.

Living Van *Plate 49*

This illustration is a living van of the type used by constructors, engineers and other workmen when working at sites remote from hotels or camps or when it was necessary to be continually on the move.

In the study of vehicles it is often difficult to draw a definite line between the caravan and the living van when it is used for permanent or temporary living, in the course of work or for pleasure, or define it by way of its user be he gypsy, showman, travelling tinker, surveyor or holidaymaker. In the horse-drawn era there were many varieties of vehicles.

The living van as distinct from the gypsy caravan would seem to date from as late as the 1880's when author and cyclist W. G. Stables decided to equip himself more completely than he could on his bicycle and ordered a lavish living van named 'Wanderer' from the Bristol Wagon Company. With its long body, clerestory roof, and sash windows complete with shutters, the mahogany panelled 'van tipped the scales at nearly 2 tons when ready for the road. Through his experience with this original vehicle he prepared a specification for the ideal travelling van for pleasure, and during the beginning of the twentieth century others followed his example and took to touring in caravans as they became popularly known. From these beginnings sprang the Caravan Club with its tens of thousands of members today using the motor and trailer versions.

From the gypsy caravans and large living vans sprang the heavy showman's living vans which marked the other end of the scale to the light towing caravans. The showmen's vehicles were the best equipped, with all sorts of fitments to render life on the road more bearable, and indeed luxurious in some instances with rich carving, fine panelling, heavy bevelled mirrors and other rich appointments.

A living van of the type illustrated would be fitted out in a reasonable manner to ensure a comfortable existence for its occupants; usually one room for sitting and eating which by simple alteration doubled as sleeping accommodation, and a second room for cooking and washing with a toilet in a corner cupboard. Storage cupboards and racks filled available spaces and a bath was sometimes provided being let into the floor and covered with a removable cover.

The name buggy actually originated in England towards the end of the eighteenth century when it was used to describe a phaeton or chaise type of cart which had a seat for one person, similar to the sulky.

The American design of buggy seems to have had its origins in the old style of German wagon and G. A. Thrupp described it as 'a light shallow tray, suspended above a slight perch carriage on two grasshopper springs, placed horizontally and parallel with and above the front and hind axle tree; on the tray one or two seats were placed, the whole was light and inexpensive, and well adapted to a new rough country without good roads.'

There were probably more buggies built than any other type of vehicle, and if the slight variations are taken into account there must have been more varieties than the 100 odd years the vehicles were produced.

Although the buggy was essentially a simple vehicle in its basic form it was still not the most stark, this qualification being reserved for the buckboard which was purely a seat placed on a long spring plank clamped to the two axles.

From the early part of the nineteenth century when the vehicle first appeared up to about 1920 when production virtually ceased there were endless varieties produced in hundreds of buggy factories over the United States. Cincinnati was the centre of the carriage building trade and at one time there were nearly eighty factories turning out vehicles there alone! There is no possible way of discovering exactly how many buggies were produced but figures for output in some particular years are interesting. Many of the manufacturers quoted outputs of 10,000 units a year in the hey-day of production around the turn of the century. Referring again to Cincinnati, it is reported that output in 1901 was 130,000 vehicles, a high proportion of which were buggies, runabouts and other light wagons. Another report quotes the number of carriages in use in the U.S.A. in 1905 as 125 million.

One famous manufacturer was the Studebaker Brothers Mfg Co. which built up a great business building wagons for the military. In 1895 it became the world's largest producer of vehicles when production reached 75,000 horse-drawn vehicles. This far sighted company built its first horse-less carriage in 1897 and horse vehicle production ceased in 1919.

With so many firms engaged in buggy production the competition was fierce and ways were always being sought to cut production costs. Prices varied widely with $35.00 being an average figure. In 1899 one builder was advertizing an open buggy for as little as $21.95 with a leather topped version at $29.90. This was at a time when a Surrey was quoted as costing $59.90.

Reference to the list of vehicle names given later in this volume shows a few of the name varieties given to differing designs of buggy. The most simple was the original square tray shape of body and this was worked upon by some builders to produce more attractive shapes with rounded corners and carvings or added mouldings. Variations in the shape of the body produced the coal box and coal scuttle varieties, the tub body shape and the curved bottom and ogee shapes. Changes in suspension were brought about by side springs, elliptic springs, torsion springs or no springs at all. The seat came in for a lot of variation too with stick seats, caned seats, jump seats, deep buttoned seats, curved seats, metal seats and automobile seats.

Brougham *Plate 51*

Shown in this illustration is one of the last types of coachmen driven carriages to be designed, the Brougham so named after Lord Brougham.

Evidently he had previously been using a one-horse chariot but, desiring something more comfortable looked around at some of the Clarence designs of the period which gave him some ideas as to how his new carriage should look. According to G. A. Thrupp writing in 1877 'Mr David Davies introduced some shapes and Messrs Laurie and Marner perfected them. I think it was in 1839 that the first vehicle which was nearly the shape of the present Brougham, was built by Mr Robinson, of Mount Street, for Lord Brougham'. He goes on to say that his company, Messrs Thrupp, built one in 1840 and that within a few years nearly all the coachbuilders were producing them, and they proved extremely popular. Dimensions of about 4 ft long and 4 ft wide are given for the body and the wheels were 2 ft 11 in. and 3 ft 7 in. high. There was no arch in the bottom line to allow the forecarriage to lock under and there were no steps to the body. It was suspended on elliptic springs at the front and five springs at the rear.

Naturally many variations appeared. The pill box had a straight front pillar and was shortened at the front to look light. The single was a light type for two people with one horse in the shafts, while the double was for a pair with seating for four.

The round front or bow front style had a pair of curved glasses at the front, a feature which also appeared on some designs of Hansom.

Char-a-banc *Plate 52*

Of French origin the name char-a-banc brings back to many the memory of a day out in the country or to the seaside in a large vehicle with bench type seats arranged across the vehicle and sometimes tiered to afford uninterrupted views of the road.

The char-a-banc like many other vehicles of the period came in a variety of shapes and sizes with seating capacities varying accordingly. Before me as I write there is a French design of 1902 which with its capacity of six including the driver has the appearance of an American style of phaeton, while another drawing dated 1909 and emanating from Australia describes a vehicle carrying twenty-four passengers as a char-a-banc or drag. Another 1909 design, this time from England, shows a three seat layout for twelve passengers describing the vehicle as an American Surrey or a char-a-banc phaeton, while other designs show there to be a great similarity between vehicles named char-a-banc, break, drag and wagonette brake. One splendid design originating in Paris in 1884 depicts a neat little vehicle with longitudinal seats, rear door, a fixed roof with roll up side curtains, and a folding hood for the driver, and of course it is a char-a-banc!

Like many other body styles the char-a-banc continued well into the motor age and in Britain they were affectionately known as 'charas' and proved extremely popular in giving untold numbers of people many pleasurable trips to the seaside. During the 1920's it became popular to fit folding hoods and the title 'all weather coaches' applied to them.

Trolley and Lift Van *Plate 53*

The combination of a flat vehicle with a detachable lift van or container gave the contractor a high degree of flexibility in operation compared with that of a conventional van.

The lift vans or sling vans or skips as they were sometimes called could be constructed to a variety of designs to suit particular purposes. For the removal contractor a plain box van with hinged end doors was adequate because mounted on the flat trolley he was able to use it as a conventional van. In fact some contractors had a flat trolley with a well in the floor so the complete vehicle was of similar capacity to a pantechnicon (see Plate 2). This well had a drop door to the rear for loading.

The lift van was moved off the flat trolley by means of an overhead crane or gantry which was fitted with four chains and hooks to connect with the eyes in the upper ends of the lifting straps or sling irons as they were called. These irons were of $2\frac{1}{4}$ in. × $\frac{1}{2}$ in. flat iron and usually extended obliquely down the sides of the van and extended under the floor so that the weight of the van was taken by the floor and not the roof as one might suppose.

Some vans were constructed with side doors for ease of unloading and if the position of these doors interfered with the angle of the sling irons then the iron would have to be fitted further apart from the centre, and may even have been vertical, bolted through the standards of the van particularly where they had fragile side panels.

For long distance removals the lift van could be placed on a flat railway wagon and arrangements made with a contractor at the destination to collect the lift van and effect the unloading.

For overseas removals the lift van was particularly useful and the one shown in the illustration was of this type being in the service of Maple's & Co. the famous London store who utilized the cross channel steamers for lift vans going to their depot in France.

Meat cartage firms were great users of lift vans and for this traffic the van was of double skin construction with a layer of insulating material between the outside boarding and the inner lining. These insulated vans were invaluable to the meat contractor because by using his horses on a shuttle basis he was able to leave a number of vans at the dockside for rapid unloading of the ship and then move them to the market as horses were available.

A specification for a panelled or diagonally boarded lift van gives overall dimensions as ranging between 11 ft 6 in. to 17 ft long according to requirements. Width is 6 ft 3 in. and height at centre of roof 6 ft 6 in. The framing is carried out in

$4\frac{1}{2}$ in. × $2\frac{1}{2}$ in. for the main sides, $2\frac{1}{2}$ in. × $2\frac{1}{2}$ in. for the summers, $4\frac{1}{2}$ in. × $2\frac{1}{2}$ in. for the ear-breadths back and front, front pillars 4 in. × 4 in. and hind pillars 6 in. × $2\frac{1}{2}$ in., all in oak. Roof is framed in ash 2 in. thick with the front and hind rails being curved from 6 in. to 10 in. at the centre and the other roof ribs being $2\frac{1}{4}$ in. deep. Roof is match boarded with $\frac{5}{8}$ in. thick boards and covered with good quality canvas well painted.

If the sides are single panelled then standards are 2 in. × 2 in. but for double panels $\frac{7}{8}$ in. × 2 in.

In the case of an insulated meat van the whole body was constructed of two layers with a 5 in. space between for the insulation in the roof, sides and ends with a 2 in. space between the inner and outer floors. As the van was being constructed all joints would be well covered with marine glue after which the panels would be covered with thick insulating paper. After the insulation of cork, felt or silicate of cotton was effected another layer of paper would be added before the covering panels were fixed.

Fire Engine *Plate 54*

Although much as been written about the speed and glamour of the old stage coaches and mail coaches, another sphere of horse transport that comes a close second regarding speed and danger although slightly less glamorous is that of the fire engine.

Fire engines developed from the early buckets and squirts, to manual pumping engines pulled first by men and later by horses, and then to horse-drawn steam powered pumps.

These powerful pumps originated in 1829 when Braithwaite & Ericsson in England built their first steam fire engine soon to be followed by a design by Hodge who in 1841 produced the first self-propelled steam fire engine in America.

At Crystal Palace in 1863 the International Exhibition

attracted entries from both sides of the Atlantic for a competition of fire engines, Britain being represented by Merryweather, Shand Mason, William Roberts and Gray & Son while the four American entrants were machines by Lee & Larner and the Amoskeag Co.

During the following 50 years the steam fire engine was to develop into a powerful and efficient machine being used by firefighters in all parts of the world. In Britain it was Merryweather and Shand Mason who built the majority of machines while the American industry was dominated by Amoskeag, Button, Gould, Silsby and American La France.

The machines were kept at the ready with a fire laid in the grate and the harness hanging from a series of ropes, hooks and pulleys suspended from the ceiling. When the alarm sounded the horses were quickly harnessed, the fire lighted and the machine driven off as fast as possible to the scene of the fire.

At the end of the nineteenth century attempts were made in both Britain, America and Germany to improve the early designs of self propelled steamers but with limited success because of the great weight of the resulting vehicles. Some of the horse-drawn steamers were converted by putting a petrol engined front wheel drive unit in place of the forecarriage while another improvization was to superimpose the fifth wheel on to the rear of a motor driven chassis so producing an articulated fire engine. Still other steamers finished their days being towed behind a motor lorry so great was the faith of the firefighters in their pumping ability.

Our illustration shows an American steamer at full gallop towards a fire with a stoker at the rear trying to get sufficient steam up ready for pumping duties upon arrival at the fire.

Cocking Cart *Plate 55*

As the dog cart name is derived from a vehicle used for carrying dogs so the cocking cart was originally a style of vehicle used to carry fighting cocks.

In the course of time the original use of the vehicles disappears but the general basic design continues for other uses. In this case the cocking cart was liked for being rather risky to drive and was easy of being overturned even in the hands of an experienced driver. With its large wheels, high body and pair of good horses it was considered just the thing for a turn of speed to overtake everything in sight and impress your friends.

A design for a particular type of cocking cart is shown in the illustration and this vehicle is unusual by virtue of having two poles for three horses abreast. Being capable of carrying six people the cart was well constructed and turned the scales at 750 lbs. Overall it measured 18 ft 3 in. long, 6 ft 4 in. wide and 9 ft 6 in. high to the top of the seat backs! With such a high centre of gravity when fully loaded the body designer was put to great pains in calculating the position of the axle in order to maintain a reasonable balance. He also had to bear in mind the imbalance caused by variations in the number of passengers and the effects of going uphill as well as the weight to be borne by the horses.

Like many other two-wheeled vehicles the back seat was arranged on sliders to help correct the balance according to the load, because in addition to passengers there was an iron ladder, horn case, umbrella case and picnic hamper located at the rear.

In this design the bodybuilder calculated that with most of the weight being at the rear a fair compromise was to position the axle almost mid way along the body floor and so the 5 ft 7 in. high wheels just about cover the 5 ft 11 in. long body (7 ft 7 in. over footboard). He calculated that it was reasonable for the horses to carry about 125 lbs between them, and this provided a safety margin to prevent the cart being tilted as a person entered at the rear or when being driven uphill.

The weight of the poles was taken by the two outside horses and broad leather straps were used to attach the poles to the harness to prevent any undue rise in the poles which might allow the cart to tilt backwards.

Ralli-Car *Plate 56*

The ralli-car appeared toward the end of the nineteenth century, its style of curving side boards being easily recognized, but there seems no apparent reason for the origin of the name.

The basic features of the car were the graceful outward curving boards which acted as splashers, and the positioning of the shafts inside the body. Like so many other varieties of car or cart the ralli-car was a descendant or variation of the dog cart and there were literally dozens of variants each with their own little difference which prompted builders to search for a new name. Looking at various references I have found a drawing of a ralli-car with its distinctive curved boards but with the shafts *outside* the body. Another design, dated 1899 shows a vehicle with the same 'ralli' curved sides but it has shafts and dasher similar to a Hansom and is plainly titled a two wheel car.

Yet another 1899 specification shows the side panels made up of alternate slats of different coloured woods and gives it the title of bent panel slatted car, but goes on to mention that it is closely related to the ralli-car and might be called a cob cart by some and a driving cart by others! Other specifications gave similar vehicles names such as Canterbury car, trilby, panel or lady's driving car, all very confusing.

Curricle *Plate 57*

The origin of the curricle is said by some to date back to an early British design of war chariot which the Romans saw, liked and copied.

During the middle ages the vehicle had been much used in Italy and underwent changes in the way the body was suspended on leather braces and its positioning in relation to the length of the shafts. In the French designs it became suspended on steel springs and during its popularity in England from about 1700 to 1840 it appeared in various styles including hooded, ogee curved body, and a steel bar across the backs of the two horses to make it safer.

Some designs had a single rumble seat for a groom in case his services were required if the horses got restless because the two horses were attached to the pole and could exert leverage and upset the occupants if not controlled.

In the type of curricle illustrated the straight bar across the two horses has been replaced with a design of curved steel springs which provide a more flexible coupling for the horses. Most curricles were driven to two horses but in this design two poles and three horses are utilized which results in a more showy appearance. With a three horses abreast troika team it was necessary to fit an extra pole socket and swingle tree as well as the extra pole. The curved steel spring attached to poles and outer horses was said to make for an easier ride because there was much more give in the connections and horse movements were not automatically conveyed to the vehicle.

Britzschka *Plate 58*

The britzschka originated in Germany and was a private travelling carriage with facilities for sleeping. It was a light vehicle with a seat for three, but when the design was brought across the English Channel in about 1820 it acquired all sorts of additions and alterations so as to make it heavier and larger.

The design was capable of considerable variation but the britzschka was basically a travelling carriage with two seats, having an ample folding head over the rear seat, and carried on a perch and C-springs with a rumble seat for servants and driven from the box or by postillion.

If required for sleeping then the front seat had to be removed or at least the capacity limited to two persons. The ample folding head has already been mentioned but this was further increased by an extension or calash which extended further forward. In addition there was a removable glass shutter or windscreen which closed the gap between the folding top and the hinged knee flap so rendering the occupants snug during inclement weather. For maximum utilization of the interior the folding steps were mounted outside the body.

For long journeys involving a large amount of luggage the britzschka was ideal. The box could be removed and replaced with a series of fitted trunks and imperials extending from the footboard to the front door pillar, the last trunk being fitted on the top of the folded down knee flap. If the servants could travel on horse back there was space for further trunks on the standard at the rear or failing this arrangement the underneath of the rumble seat could provide further storage.

The britzschka was really a variation of the basic barouche design adopted for long distance travel. A further variation was the dormeuse which quickly followed the britzschka as a popular travelling carriage, this design differing by way of having a fixed head coupé style body with an extended front enabling the occupants to lie full length within. Fitted trunks over this extension helped with the luggage capacity which was further enhanced by the fitted imperials carried on the fixed head.

Paraffin Tanker *Plate 59*

During the first few years of this century when the motor car was in its infancy it was possible to witness the delivery of petrol to garages by horse-drawn vehicles. In those early days before petrol was stored in underground tanks and dispensed by roadside pumps it was handled from local depot to garage and on to customer in the 2-gallon can. It was not long however before the the oil companies realized that it was not in their interests to deliver petrol in this way and soon the motive power of the vehicle was of the 'horse-less' variety.

The delivery of paraffin or kerosene was somewhat different because it went to a wide variety of outlets each having different arrangements for their storage tanks. It was not so highly inflammable as petrol so needed less stringent regulations concerning its storage. Most of the dealers dispensed their lamp oil to customers who also came along to purchase their other household requirements such as flour, saucepans, rice, pegs, beans and soda. In some stores all these items were in close juxtaposition which did not help matters at all!

In some areas the dealers were enterprising enough to have their own tanker which they filled either at the local bulk storage depot, usually in the railroad yard or from their own storage tanks.

Tanks varied in size from about 200 gallons mounted on a two-wheel cart frame up to 600 gallons on four wheels and drawn by a pair.

A typical specification for a 600 gallon tank gives the dimensions of the vessel as being 7 ft 9 in. long by 3 ft 11 in. diameter and made from 10 gauge iron. A filling flange and cover is at the top and an emptying cock is situated at the rear bottom of the tank. All joints are caulked and closely rivetted.

To support the tank a frame consisting of two $4\frac{1}{2}$ in. $\times$ 3 in longitudinals suitably crossbraced with similar material or iron tie rods is made. At the point where the weight of the tank and its contents meet the frame some form of packing is provided to prevent serious damage to the tank. This being either felt, leather or suitably angled timber fillets. The tank is secured laterally by metal strapping and endwise movement is prevented by a crossboard at the rear and the driver's seat or cab at the front.

A box is provided around the outlet cock at the rear to house the various measures, act as a drip tray and can be fitted with locking doors to prevent unauthorised use. A length of metal protected rubber/canvas or leather hose would be carried for bulk discharge and there may be a semi-rotary hand pump for 'non-gravity' discharges. Wheels are 3 ft 0 in. and 4 ft 2 in. high and a mechanical footbrake acts on the offside rear wheel.

The illustration shows a 600 gallon paraffin tanker from around the 1900 period complete with coachbuilt cab which was comparatively comfortable compared with the more usual arrangement of a folding hood or just nothing at all!

Railway Van *Plate 60*

Up until about 1920 the railways in Britain enjoyed the position of being the premier mode of transport for goods over long distances. With their main lines radiating from the capital linking the major centres of industry and commerce and the branch lines connecting up the less important towns and trading centres there were lines within a few miles of most places originating traffic. Their best customers were naturally rail-linked with loading banks or private sidings and some even had their own privately-owned wagons to carry their products.

For the thousands of other customers who had no transport of their own it meant that the collection or delivery of goods by train had to be carried out by a very large fleet of railway owned road vehicles or appointed railways cartage agents. So the railways became good customers of the well-known van and cart builders or else they went ahead and built their own using the skills of their carriage and wagon building personnel.

The pair horse delivery van shown in the illustration is of a type built by the old established firm of G. Scammell and

Nephew of Spitalfields, London, for the Metropolitan Railway in 1912. This firm of bodybuilders and engineers was established in 1837 and produced all manner of vehicles for private and business use from small butchers' carts to private drags. As the horse-drawn era started to decline they turned their attention to building bodies for motor vehicles and used their metal working skills for building trailers. Motor vehicle enthusiasts will have noted the Scammell name and probably already guessed that one of the directors was instrumental in designing the first truly matched articulated lorry. A new factory was built at Watford in Hertfordshire for the production of lorries and it was a separate entity from the Spitalfields concern.

Returning to the railway delivery vehicles, the type of vehicle illustrated in the London area was called a van and in fact the general design was known as a London van although variations on the theme were known as contractors' vans when operated by haulage contractors or jobmasters or carriers as they were called.

The vans were really the mainstay of the railway cartage fleet being of both single and pair-horse types. They were used to handle all manner of merchandise except for the small fragile parcels which were conveyed in lighter covered tilt vans, and the heavier, larger and more specialized pieces of equipment which required rather special types of vehicle.

Ragman's Trolley *Plate 61*

In many parts of Britain one can still see one type of vehicle that has really never gone out of use – the old ragman's trolley. It goes under many titles and appears in a variety of guises. Some may call it a totter's cart, others say it is a second-hand dealer's cart, older members of the family remember it affectionately as the rag and bone man's cart, while the younger element regard it as a diddicoy's cart. Whatever title you choose for the vehicle it probably reflects more of the owner's present pursuit rather than of the job for which the vehicle was originally designed. Today's vehicles often show signs of previous owners and uses. They may have started life as a greengrocer's or fruiterer's cart, they may have originally been used by a baker or dairy or perhaps by an earlier relative for some small business.

Whatever their ancestry they are usually small vehicles and on pneumatic tyres. Bodywork is usually of the flat variety with perhaps low sides or at least a sideboard which once proudly displayed the owner's name. Their haunts are the parts of towns and cities where anything may be thrown away as rubbish or scrap. It all depends on what is being thrown away or what is worth being retrieved at that particular time. You may see the turnout (if one can call it that) moving at a gentle pace along a suburban road with the owner sitting easily at the side of the cart ringing a handbell or shouting some unintelligible word at about every tenth step that the horse takes. The horse plods at a steady pace as though on a treadmill, content to amble along in his ill fitting harness until being asked to wait for a moment by a word uttered by his master. The horse might be left to his own devices while according to his habit the owner haggles the price for an old bicycle or mangle from a householder who has heard his call. If the cart boasts the new-fangled motor car axles with internal expanding brakes, then the poor old horse might get stopped in his tracks by a sudden boot on the brake pedal, before the driver is off to look for scrap from a demolition site or lift some old electrical fittings from a roadside skip. So the day goes on, with perhaps a couple of stops near a cafe or outside a dealer's yard while a deal is done, and on those occasions the wheels are scotched with a brick and the bait sack taken off the cart and put down at the horse's head.

Undoubtedly the most famous English dealer's horse has

been Hercules immortalized in the BBC TV series of Steptoe and Son. In this comedy programme the wide variety of stuff collected by these general dealers is faithfully portrayed in scenes of the yard where a stuffed bear literally rubs shoulders with an old skeleton and baths, basins, boilers, bedsteads and bicycles abound on every side.

Produce Van *Plate 62*

Described in the original specification as a produce van the vehicle shown in this illustration was a French design of 1908 appearing originally in La Carrosserie Française.

Overall the vehicle was 15 ft long, 6 ft 6 in. wide and 7 ft 10 in. over the seat. Within these dimensions the upper part of the body, which projected over the wheels, was 11 ft 5 in. long, 6 ft 6 in. wide and 1 ft 4½ in. high. To the rear of the forecarriage the body dropped into a commodious well measuring 7 ft 8 in. long, 4 ft 2 in. wide and 2 ft 6 in. deep, the floor of which was a little over a foot from the ground. Wheels were 3 ft and 2 ft 10 in. high and the side springs 4 ft 6 in. long at the centres both front and rear. An inverted half elliptic spring was connected to the rear ends of the forecarriage springs.

In order to achieve a body as wide as this the rear wheels were made small so as not to project beyond the upper body sides. Had they been larger it would have meant an overall width of something like 8 ft which would have precluded the vehicle from general use! As it was, the design was not recommended for any but city roads by an Australian reviewer who unfortunately was a little generous with his Imperial measurement conversion table and reported that the vehicle was 7 ft 6 in. wide!

The massive curved irons supporting the rear springs are worthy of note, adding a typical French flourish as well as being perfectly functional. In fact the whole vehicle was built on straightforward lines with nothing too fancy, but with just a hint of decoration to take the edge off what was really just an ordinary market van. The curving seat supports were not too extravagant and the row of small spindles between the middle and top rails on the upper part of the body provided a pleasant lightening effect.

Sensible features of the design were an adequately plated well section and full height rear doors. The longitudinal floor boards were laid with 1 in. gaps so that wet produce could drain en route and the low floor height made market unloading simpler.

Returning once again to the Australian report, the reviewer mentioned that the already large body could have a covered top added and so be converted into a furniture van or a useful van for handling light bulky goods.

Moving Van *Plate 63*

The American style of moving van for use with three horses abreast is shown in this illustration. An interesting comparison of styles can be made by reference to the British version shown in Plate 2.

The American vehicle was a lofty affair with quite a long body, the rear axle being placed near to the rear which resulted in virtually no rear overhang. However, like all good removal vans there was a capacious tailboard which could be used, and the bodybuilder provided rope ties on both rear body pillars so that the overhanging load could be secured.

The carrying area of the body was roughly rectangular with the substantial driver's box being cantilevered out at the front. Secure handrails and footboards were provided to assist the driver to surmount his lofty perch, a position which put him well above the backs of his horses.

Mr Turner used the large billboard size van sides to advantage announcing to all that the world moved and so did he, but he did not say that he did world removals as one imagines from the first impression.

Gospel Wagon *Plate 64*

One of the more unusual vehicles is undoubtedly the gospel wagon which was taken from a Hub design of 1887.

Sub-titled the chapel-on-wheels this vehicle was constructed by Pearce and Lawton of Washington DC for the Central Union Mission and replaced an old omnibus which was unsuited for the purpose of open air gospel meetings for a variety of reasons.

The design prepared by Pearce and Lawton closely followed the mission's desire for a vehicle to seat up to forty persons on moveable benches, to have room for an organ, and to have facilities for speakers to be near the standing audience and protected from the sun.

The body of the completed vehicle measured some 20 ft in length, was 7 ft wide and 6 ft 8 in. high. Access was by means of folding steps at the rear end where a hinged door was provided. Seating was afforded by four 8 ft long benches trimmed in leather, these being arranged along the sides of the vehicle for travelling but were capable of being reversed so that the occupants all sat facing the audience on one side when a meeting was in progress. A stout fold down platform was arranged in the centre of one side for the speaker and a folding canopy protected him from the sun. In the middle of the body, behind the speaker's platform, the organ was sited.

The vehicle was carried on 3 ft high Warner pattern wheels and when loaded was drawn by four horses.

Ambulance *Plate 65*

The amublance has appeared in many guises and sizes including very sparse military types, plain covered carts, beautifully finished private types, secret Brougham styles, special children's types and open cattle cart designs.

The simplest were merely adaptations of other vehicles where a sick person was given some comfort by being placed on cushions or perhaps a stretcher on the floor of the vehicle. Next came the purely functional kind probably used by the military, these being a plain canvas covered wagon with folding seats for sitting patients or for a lying down casualty. By folding up the seats to the sides there would be room for two stretcher cases on the floor. A fixed seat would be provided at the front inside of the body for the attendant and a plain cupboard would house simple bandages and dressings. When not required the stretchers would be rolled up and stored under the seats or strapped to the sides. Our illustration depicts an American military pair horse ambulance with drop steps at rear and roll up canvas sides.

Another simple type for hot climates would have canvas curtain sides which could be rolled up in hot weather while the remaining wire mesh sides would help to keep out flies while not restricting the passage of air. There would be a folding seat for the attendant and alongside this a couple of slides and extension rails to take a fixed frame type of stretcher with curled horsehair mattress in two parts complete with means of elevating one end if required. An adequate first aid kit was stowed beneath the driver's seat.

Getting more sophisticated some ambulances took on the appearance of a private omnibus with opaque glass windows, full height doors at the rear and a cranked axle to allow for easy access by walking patients while providing sufficient headroom for the stretcher cases placed one above the other on special framework with secure fixings to the side.

One German style had a door at the side for the walking patients while the rear stretcher entrance was divided horizontally and the lower flap used as a guide for the stretcher which was mounted on a metal framework and manoeuvred into its housing by a two-wheeled trolley.

Another interesting design was that of the Brougham ambulance, which as the name suggests looked for all the world a Brougham but in fact was an ambulance cunningly designed to appear as a normal carriage of the day. A flat floor was provided to take a stretcher and a seat for an attendant was provided alongside. The back of the carriage was made to hinge down level with the floor for loading the stretcher and adequate length was obtained by running the stretcher right forward under the driving boot; this allowed the rear hinged portion to be closed up and the normal carriage impression to go undisturbed. Ideally the side glasses should be glazed with blue or opaque glass to thwart curious glances and in some designs the Brougham was of the extension front type with Venetian slats in place of glasses.

Other types of ambulance included some specially designed for young children these being fitted with shorter stretchers and lower seats as well as a toy cupboard! Our friend the horse was sick himself sometimes and had to be transported; hence the need for horse ambulances which could be as simple as a two-wheeled cattle cart with drop tailboard, or the more complete four wheel kind with roof over for protection, padded interior, overhead gantry and winch for loading, side rails and body belt for support and detachable lamps for illumination.

Funeral Hearse *Plate 66*

This plate shows the later style of hearse or casket car which was used until the advent of motor hearses. Prior to this, the type of vehicle used was extremely depressing, consisting of a large black box on wheels which, complete with its black horses and nodding black plumes did nothing to relieve the gloom of a burial.

Many funeral processions were of the walking variety

because most burials were in local churchyards, but after the passing of the Public Health and Public Burial Acts during the middle of the nineteenth century, and with the setting up of large scale cemeteries some distance from the towns, the vehicular procession was necessary.

After much agitation from those concerned about a slightly brighter form of transport for the dead, various designs of hearse began to appear. As in our illustration these were really a large and elegant glass case into which the coffin or casket was placed together with any special covering or restrained decoration that the relatives wished. By using purple, silver and white for the various fittings and curtains the vehicle took on a less depressing spectacle, or as one contemporary writer put it 'the vehicle befitted the silent solemnity of the occasion.'

A specification for a hearse similar to that illustrated states that the body was 7 ft 6 in. long, 4 ft 5 in. wide and 4 ft 0 in. high. The main body framing was of white ash with a $1\frac{3}{4}$ in. thick bottom frame and $1\frac{1}{4}$ in. sides. The thick bevelled glass was carefully bedded in a liberal amount of putty or some builders used rubber; wood fillets on the inside of the side frame held the glass in place. The floor of the body had several hardwood rollers to help position the coffin easily. The top decorations were of cast metal, nickel plated or in aluminium, and the hammercloth was carved out of whitewood or kauri pine and suitably decorated. Wheels were 3 ft 3 in. and 4 ft 3 in. high. In 1899 the price of such a vehicle was £136 10*s*.

Band Wagon *Plate 67*

Probably the most extravagant types of vehicles were those used by the travelling showmen who naturally wanted something to catch both the eye and the imagination of the public as they travelled the country.

Some travelling showmen were individuals who toured

alone using just one vehicle which contained their living facilities and provided space for any props needed for their performances. If a family or group toured together as a troupe then it might be necessary to have two vehicles in the group, one for living and another for a tent and equipment.

When a travelling fair or circus went on the move then all sorts of vehicles went to make up the convoy, living vans, flat trucks, cage trucks, vans, scenery vans, equipment trucks etc. Travelling showmen are past masters in the art of improvization and adaptation, and many of the vehicles were conversions and adaptions to suit particular needs.

Some of the vehicles were travelling works of art with plenty of fancy lettering and giant pictures capable of making an impact as the procession hit town. Some of the vehicles were really beautifully turned out with little regard to expense. The living vans were solidly constructed of the finest materials, very comfortably furnished, well equipped and richly ornamented with bevelled glass, fine carvings and superb paintwork. An organ van would be solidly constructed to protect its valuable cargo, richly carved and ornamented to attract its listeners and cleverly designed to provide access to the working parts for future adjustment and repair.

The illustration shows an American band wagon built for a travelling circus. The whole vehicle is covered with carvings depicting musical instruments and figures with an air of myth and legend.

Brewer's Dray *Plate 68*

The early form of transport for beer casks was that of a yoke type pole carried upon the shoulders of two draymen with the cask slung from two short chains. This was manageable for small casks up to the kilderkin or firkin size but for the larger barrels, hogsheads and butts some form of vehicle was required where the casks had to be moved some distance.

The type of transport used was a sled consisting of two stout timbers curved up at the front and joined by some equally stout cross bearers. Upon this simple frame were laid the casks and the draught animal harnessed to the front. The draymen would walk with the sled and manhandle the casks at the point of delivery.

Next came the two wheeled dray which had a straightforward frame like the sled but with the side pieces extended to form shafts. It was carried on a pair of heavy wheels 3 ft 6 in. high and 6½ in. wide shod with a double row of iron strakes. Two horses in tandem were used to draw the dray and it carried a load of three butts placed across the frame.

As the area of operation increased and the need for larger vehicles emerged the more familiar design of four wheel dray emerged. This style of body consisted of four stout longitudinals carried on six or more cross bearers.

The space between the middle pair of longitudinals was boarded for the drayman to stand on but the spaces on either side were left empty for the stowage of the casks on the roll. These casks were in fact carried on their bouge with their centres about 30 deg. to the horizontal and their heads facing out.

Other designs followed some looking similar to contractors' wagons by having part boarded or slat sides and solid floors. Another style was with a wagon type body but a boarded tilt roof curved like the top portion of a barrel top Romany caravan. This was usually painted a light colour to reflect the sun and help keep the beer cool.

Most of the surviving brewers' drays are of the wagon type probably because they are more attractive in appearance and provide greater space for advertizing the name of their owners. Purely for show purposes the pair horse drays and wagons often appear with four, six or even eight horses which makes the whole thing ridiculous.

The illustration is a German variety of brewer's dray which is considerably longer than its British and American counterparts. This is one of the vehicles used for publicity purposes appearing with a load of modern metal casks.

The vehicle is along the lines of the accepted type of dray mentioned above but with typical teutonic efficiency the space beneath the body proper is used to carry additional casks. The method of slinging these casks is not unlike the system adopted for carrying casks slung beneath a yoke as mentioned earlier and the weight of the cask itself is instrumental in the chains maintaining their grip on the chimes of the cask.

Patrol Wagon *Plate 69*

This illustration shows a design of an American police patrol wagon as used around 1912. It is built on the wagonette brake style with entrance at the rear and seats along both sides. It was for use by the cops as a patrol vehicle or for carrying a number of men to a special job or disturbance. Naturally it came in useful for bringing back persons for interrogation or to be put in jail!

In some American cities it fulfilled the dual purpose of patrol wagon and ambulance and for this use was equipped with a full size stretcher and a smaller stretcher for use on staircases. These stretchers were stowed under the side seats when not in use.

The vehicle illustrated is constructed almost entirely in ash and is roughly 9 ft long, 4 ft 3 in. wide and 6 ft high inside.

The front wheels are 3 ft 2 in. high and are carried on 3 ft 2 in. long elliptic springs while the rear wheels are 4 ft diameter and suspended on 3 ft 4 in. half elliptics.

Ice Van *Plate. 70*

In the days before small ice making machines could be obtained there was nevertheless considerable demand for ice in many trades requiring some form of cooling for their products. Ice was delivered from large ice making plants in horse-drawn vans as promptly as possible, and considerable thought was given to insulation of the vans.

In Britain when the normal summer day-time temperature was at least moderate, ice was usually carried in open carts or vans with merely sacks covering the large blocks of ice.

On the Australian continent where temperatures are much higher in some parts, the completely covered vehicle was favoured, great attention being paid to its insulation.

America as shown in the illustration tended to favour a covered vehicle to keep off the direct sunlight but the vehicle was enclosed at the rear by hinged tailboard and folding curtains.

Construction of the vehicles varied with some designs having a solid floor with just a couple of holes for drainage, while others had a slatted floor and plenty of ventilation. The closed vehicles sometimes had double panel construction to reduce the risk of temperature rise and this feature was further enhanced by placing cork insulation in the cavity. The heavy blocks of ice could soon wear the floor so some makers made the floor easily removable while others favoured zinc panelling to both floor and sides. Another important feature was the sealing of the body joints, because with a permanently wet load any small cavities would soon fill with water, swell, and eventually cause the body to rot and fall apart.

Light Trade Cart *Plate 71*

Among the horsed vehicles used by the retail trades some of the most attractive were the single and pair horse light vans used by the various shops, departmental stores and tradesmen of the day.

In each of the various trades there developed an accepted

format or style which embraced the shape of the vehicle, its colour scheme and the livery of the driver, and the quality of the horse and its harness. One became accustomed to seeing white, cream or other pale colours for the dairy trade (see Plate 29); the butcher likewise used light, clean colours (Plate 30) to perpetuate an aura of cleanliness and although laundry vans came in a variety of colours and house styles their lettering and layout were aimed at conveying an air of smartness and promptitude so necessary if they were to succeed in their business. A style of American laundry van is shown in the illustration.

Like many other local businesses in towns and cities there was often plenty of competition for the launderer, and he would use his van as a mobile billboard. The laundry vans announced to all that their establishment was a steam laundry or that all items were hand finished, or that it could guarantee a prompt service or that they had reached the dizzy heights of some form of royal patronage.

The laundry van driver was not quite in the same league as some of his friends. His was quite a heavy job with those large laundry baskets and a lot of his day was spent stopping and starting again, a burden for his horse. His van was often fully loaded for most of the day – delivering the clean and picking up the soiled, so there was no easy trot back home like so many of his friends who merely carried out a delivery function.

Spring Dray *Plate 72*

Shown in this illustration is an Australian design of vehicle termed a spring dray. It was a general purpose vehicle for a load of 10 to 15 cwt and when fitted with the windlass attachment and sloping rear platform could be used for removing dead horses from the street. This type of vehicle found use in small towns where there was not enough work for a vehicle to be kept specially for use in removing horses. A more elaborate vehicle might be used by a horse slaughterer where the turnover of horses was high, in some cases being a four wheeled type with cranked axle to produce a low floor line. Another design used a large tailboard which could be let down to provide an inclined ramp for ease of loading. Of similar design were horse ambulances which sometimes had a covered top for the protection of the occupants (horse) and a roof mounted block and tackle for hoisting up an injured animal.

In the design illustrated the body is 6 ft 6 in. long and 4 ft wide with 21 in. sides being of 12 in. wide boards with a metal rod extension. The body is framed of 3 in. × 2 in. stuff with four 5 in. × 1½ in. cross bearers and two 2 in. × 2 in. longitudinals. Floor is of 6½ in. × 1¼ in. boards laid lengthwise. Springs are 4 ft 2 in. centres and wheels 4 ft 6 in. high, 5 ft 1 in. out to out.

For use in removing horses a tapered hardwood roller was positioned just above the shafts about 15 in. in front of the body. One end of this roller was located in a removable metal pillar slotted into one shaft while the other end was positioned in a metal ratchet located likewise in the opposite shaft. A removable wooden pin was dropped into suitable holes in the roller to provide leverage for winding the rope on to the roller as the load was winched on to the body.

The sloping rear portion of the body consisted of two curved pieces 2 in. thick to which were screwed 1 in. boards. The inner ends of the curved pieces located in two metal staples bolted up under the floor of the dray.

The operation of removing a dead animal was to first remove the dray horse from the shafts. With the sloping rear platform in position the cart was tilted up close to the animal on the ground. The rope was unwound from the roller across the dray body over the sloping rear portion and tied around the animal. By operating the windlass with the ratchet in operation the carcass was drawn up on to the dray body.

When the point of balance was reached as the load balanced the shafts were held until the roller was removed and the dray horse reharnessed in the shafts.

HORSE-DRAWN VEHICLE NAMES

In the study of the horse-drawn vehicle one soon discovers that the method of naming or giving titles to different types and styles is a most complex matter. Few of the designs are clear cut and isolated. As the industry has grown over the centuries in various parts of the world so the adoption of names has expanded. Being first a localized industry it is not surprising that there has been little standardization in design or title and what one man calls a cab phaeton another will say is a Milord, and a town chariot to an Englishman may be a coupe to a Frenchman.

So it was thought that a list of titles was a must for this volume in an endeavour to try and give a clearer picture to the reader. It soon became evident that to list every name ever used was going to be difficult if not downright impossible with so many differing names for the same basic style of vehicle. With so many coachbuilders turning out their own particular style of carriage and then giving it a proper name any 'complete' list was soon going to contain so many 'one-offs' as to make it a chronicle of almost every carriage built.

In similar vein the goods carrying carts and vans are more numerous but named in a much saner fashion. Unlike their passenger carrying brothers the frieght carriers were not named after the designer, builder or customer but generally after the use to which they were to be put. Hence we find plenty of forage carts, milk floats, timber wagons and garbage wagons, although things do go a little awry with names like London van, Scotch cart and German wagon but which are accepted with a little more credulity than say an emperor phaeton.

Still wishing to include a list of names it was decided to include as many as possible without trying to trace the origins of every type of gig, buggy or phaeton that was discovered. As so many of the commercial vehicle were so obvious it was decided to exclude them almost entirely in their compound form it being felt that to list such names as brewer's dray, millers cart and railway van was superfluous.

No doubt many readers will run their fingers down my list and exclaim 'he's left out phoongyes chariot and the cross bolster side spring buggy' – yes, and I'm sorry, but I'll include them in the next volume!

GLOSSARY

Adopticon. Name given to a particular style of advertizing vehicle drawn by six horses in Chicago, 1887.

Alexandra Car. A type of pleasure cart with cut under body.

Ambulance. Derived from the French – 'moving hospital'. An amply sprung vehicle usually on four wheels with fixed or folding seats and/or provision for stretcher cases. Many varieties.

Amempton. A variety of convertible carriage invented by Edwin Kesterton in London in 1855, it being possible to remove the upper part for summer use.

Americaine. French term for the American Buggy.

Araba. A Turkish four wheeled covered carriage.

Arcera. Ancient Roman vehicle.

Band Wagon. A wagon for conveying a band which usually accompanied a travelling circus.

Bandy. A plain two wheeled flat cart with hoops and matting cover used in India.

Barco de Tierra. Early type of wagon used in South America.

Barge. An American term for a large wagonette style vehicle with seats running lengthwise

Barouche. A cut down coach consisting of under carriage and lower quarters of a coach with door with a hood over the rear seat. A four wheeled vehicle although its Italian ancestor Biroccio was two wheeled.

Bath Wagon. A variety of French wagon which carried a bath tub.

Battery Wagon. Type of army wagon for carrying tools and items of repair for artillery.

Battlesden Car. A variety of two wheeled road cart.

Beach Wagon. Term used in Eastern States for a wagon used to convey parties over the beach.

Beer Patrol Wagon. Name given to special type of beer carrying vehicle introduced by Ohlsen Wagon Co., wherein the beer kegs were carried on a revolving frame.

Benna. A Roman vehicle.

Berlin(e). Originated in Prussia as a double perch full coach suspended on throughbraces and richly carved, gilded and ornamented.

Berlinet. Small version of a Berlin.

Black & Tan. New York term applied to a cheap cab because of its colour.

Black Maria. Slang term for police van said to have originated from Maria Lee a competent lady of Boston whom the police regularly called up to help get recalcitrant troublemakers into the van.

Bolster Wagon. An American vehicle with side bars and bolsters but no side springs to give a hard suspension.

Boon Hansom. Particular style of two wheeled cab invented by Boon & Ries of London. Driver sat to one side at rear while passengers could enter at either front or rear.

Bracket Front Wagon. A type of Buggy having a bracket front to the body carried forward to form a dasher.

Brake. Large vehicles for carrying a number of passengers as well as luggage and equipment.

Break. A heavy driving vehicle with high seat originally used to 'break in' new horses to carriage use.

Breaking Cart. Lighter form of vehicle used for breaking in horses for vehicle use.

Brett. Old term for vehicle like a barouche which had some feature of the Britzschka.

Britton Wagon. Named after J. W. Britton of New York (1872); a modification of a Goddard buggy for road use.

Britzschka. A travelling or freight wagon said to have originated in Austria, Poland or Russia. Later designs made it a useful vehicle for long distance travel because of features enabling a large amount of luggage to be carried and enabling passengers to lie full length and sleep in it.

Brougham. Taking its name from Lord Brougham this type of coach is similar to the French coupé. It is a low-hung one horse vehicle with varieties such as 'single', 'double', 'bow front'.

Brougham Hansom. Patent design of cab with driver's seat at front and passenger entrance at rear by W. &. F. Thorn, London.

Brunswick. American family carriage similar to a Surrey.

Buckboard. Early type of wagon used in mountain regions of eastern United States consisting of seats bolted to long board mounted on four wheels. Motion of vehicle gave rise to name 'bucking'. Later types of buckboard wagons were of shorter wheelbase, and sometimes had springs and slatted body to increase elasticity and so give smoother ride.

Buckboard-Barouche. A term

used in the American Far West for a type of buckboard used as a stage vehicle.

Buggy. Although having American connexions the term originated in England towards the end of the eighteenth century and was originally described by Felton as being 'a cart name given to phaetons or chaise which can only contain one person or seat'. Later American styles were based on a simple box body vehicle for one or two people mounted on four wheels. There have probably been more varieties on the buggy theme than any other, and so it has proved impossible to list all the variations with their titles, however a selection is given together with other names for which no explanation has been readily found.

Buggy Variations

Amish. Name given to a style of buggy built for the Amish sect existing in Indiana, Ohio and Pennsylvania who do not use automobiles.

Auto Seat. Type made with a curved back and deep seat of the style used in automobiles of the day.

Azaline. Variety of tub bodied buggy with panelled sides.

Bonaventa. Standing top buggy of Pennsylvania.

Britton. Similar to a corning buggy but with a drop front.

Business. Style of buggy with space for merchandise.

Coal Box. Design by Brewster & Co., New York, having no top, the front cut away but high behind seat.

Coal Scuttle. Old type of coal box buggy.

Concord. Named after Concord, N.H. Had three perches and side springs.

Corning. Later form of coal box buggy with deep sides, cut down front and moulded panels, first sold to Erastus Corning of Albany.

Cut Under. Type having a cut out in the body allowing the front wheels to lock round.

Decomeo. Old style of cut under coal box buggy.

Dexter. Patent type of buggy by W. W. Igner of Hulton, P.A., incorporating his design of suspension and named after a famous trotting horse.

Duke of York. Name given to an English buggy built on the lines of a gig.

Fantail. A variation of buggy with the body cut down at the back to leave a tail at rear.

Harness. Light type of buggy for road and track use where the horse is shown in harness.

Iron-Age. Name given to an all metal vehicle of about 1870 that did not achieve any popularity because of incurable rattling.

Jagger. A variation of square box buggy carried on side bars and bolsters without springs.

Lawrence. Style produced by J. W. Lawrence of New York City.

Monitor. A variation of square box buggy with a sunken bottom and concave sides.

Ogee. Old style of buggy with the bottom in the ogee shape.

Piano Box. A variation of square box buggy having rounded corners.

Scoop. Side spring buggy with a scoop shape.

Tray Body. An early form of buggy by Watson of Philadelphia resembling a richly carved tray.

Whitechapel. Style of buggy with the stick seat in the fashion of a Whitechapel cart.

Yacht. An improvement on the tray body buggy with lines somewhat akin to a yacht.

Buggyette. A particular design of Buggy built in Calcutta, India.

Cab. Abbreviation of cabriolet which has become synonymous with the Hackney carriage or taxi as a vehicle for public hire.

Cabriolet. French term said to be derived from the Italian two wheel gig or Carriuolo with long springy shafts and nautilus shell style body. After being used as the street hack in France the English took on the style in the early nineteenth century and it later appeared as the four wheeled cabriolet-phaeton. In Europe it later became the Milord. Latest style was a vehicle on four wheels, low with hood but no door and with panelled driver's seat.

Caisson. A military vehicle for carrying ammunition.

Calache. Late eighteenth century European coach with folding heads similar to the canoe landau.

Calash. Name given to a vehicle originating in the mid nineteenth century as a coach with folding hood at the rear quarters and a door in two halves. Peculiar to America.

Calesa. A type of one horse vehicle used in Philippines.

Calesso. An Italian two wheel hooded vehicle.

California Wood Spring Wagon. Variety of coalbox buggy with wooden springs and thoroughbraces introduced about 1867 in San Francisco.

Car. From the Latin *carrus* – a four wheeled carriage. Term often used in place of cart such as ralli-car, governess car, etc.

Cars and Carts. In many instances these terms are synonomous, being used to describe very similar vehicles. As with the phaeton, the gig and the buggy there have been innumerable variations and it is an exhausting task trying to discover all the names that have existed. The family of carts has spread into the realm of commercial vehicles in a wide array of sizes and types including both two and four wheel configurations each with its own particular use, and of course title. The carts for private use were named mostly after the area, builder or customer, while those for trade use usually took their name from what they carried or the calling of their owner.

Alexandra; Battlesden; Bedford; Malvern; Moray; Newport; Norwich; Pagnell; Tandem; Whitechapel.

Canoe Landau. Style of landau where the bottom line was a graceful sweeping curve as opposed to the earlier square cut quarter landau.

Cape Cart. Originated in South Africa. A road cart with hood and canvas top.

Caravan. Originally name for a wagon with a covered top for carrying both goods and passengers. Later used to describe vehicles used by travelling and nomadic people.

Cardinal Coach. A coach for the use of cardinals, painted red.

Carpentum. Originally a Roman two wheeled, covered top vehicle. Later used as name for a vehicle produced in England about 1830.

Carrack. Old term for a large covered wagon.

Carreta/Carretela. A two-horsed covered cab used in the Philippines although the term has been used in Italy, Spain and Portugal.

Carriage. Originally used to describe almost any kind of vehicle for passengers. Later technically used for the undercarriage or frame, axle and wheels which carry the body.

Carriagem. Portuguese term for small cart.

Carrinho. Portuguese term for cart.

Carri-Coche. Early type of two wheeled passenger vehicle used in South America.

Carriole. French two wheeled

covered carriage or cart.

Carro de Boes. Primitive cart of the Azores.

Carrocin. Portuguese term for small cart.

Carrocio. An Italian four wheeled cart.

Carruca. A Roman vehicle.

Carryall. Local term of New England for a Rockaway having curtain sides and being used to convey a whole family.

Cart. Very old term for a vehicle which was not a carriage and usually therefore much more rough in construction. Latterly used to describe simple two wheeled vehicles both freight carrying (tip cart, water cart) and passenger varieties (Ralli-cart, Whitechapel cart).

Catafalque. Italian style of funeral car having open sides decorated with paintings or sculptures.

Chair. Old name for a light carriage similar to chaise.

Chaise. Term applied to a light vehicle almost universally on two wheels which originally consisted of a seat on a light framework with particularly springy shafts.

Chamulcus. A Roman vehicle.

Char-a-Banc. French term for a vehicle with long seats. Usually applied to vehicles carrying a large number of passengers on cross benches.

Charat. Ancient vehicle of France and Italy.

Chariot. One of the earliest names of wheeled vehicles going back to Greek, Roman and Egyptian times. Later used to describe the high slung carriages of England in the early nineteenth century.

Chatelaine. New York coach-builder's name for a type of Stanhope gig.

Chihuahua. Mexican term for a heavy type of travelling wagon.

Chilese Car. Primitive cart of Chile.

Cisium. A two wheeled Roman vehicle.

Clarence. A coach with curved glass front, fully panelled body with elliptic springs at the front and both elliptic and C-springs at the rear. Named in honour of the Duke of Clarence.

Coach. Said to be derived from the Hungarian town of Kotze where the type of vehicle originated; the term coach is generally accepted as applying to a closed vehicle with fixed head, doors and *windows*.

Coachee. American coach of the mid nineteenth century used mainly in the southern states.

Cocking Cart. A high seat two

wheeler with a small box body for carrying fighting cocks.

Concord. Originated from Concord, New Hampshire; a substantial coach of the thorough-brace type.

Conestoga Wagon. Early American travelling wagon introduced at the end of the eighteenth century.

Corbillard. French term for a hearse.

Costermonger's Cart. Originally a term applied to a cart used by English apple sellers. Later used to include all kinds of carts used by peddlars.

Coupé. Derived from the French – to cut. Term originally used to denote cut down coach bodies. Later used to signify a vehicle similar to a Brougham but larger. When of increased capacity it became a Clarence.

Coupelet. Term used to denote a small coupé with calache top instead of the panelled top.

Covina. Old type of war chariot with scythes.

Crystal Car. Name given to glass sided street cab of New York City about 1876.

Curate Cart. A particular type of small two wheeled cart.

Curras. A Roman chariot.

Curricle. Originally a Roman vehicle. Latterly used to describe a type of two wheeled vehicle similar to a gig but drawn by two horses and being particularly elaborate and showy. The unusual harnessing arrangement included a bar across the backs of the horses which carried the weight of the pole.

Democrat Wagon. A square box open vehicle like a large buggy with four moveable seats.

Depot Wagon. A square box vehicle for both passengers and luggage.

Derby. French style of four wheel vehicle similar to a dog cart.

Diable. A French vehicle of the eighteenth century similar to a coupelet.

Diligence. Large type of road coach much used for long distance travel in mainland Europe.

Dioropha. A mid nineteenth century design of carriage which could be used either open or closed, the top part being detachable for summer use. Type of landau patented by James Rock of London in 1851.

Disobligeant/Disobliger. A variety of small chaise for one person only popular in France in the eighteenth century.

Dog Cart. Originally a two wheeled cart for carrying shooting dogs it later became a term loosely applied to all manner of light carts.

Dolgusha. A Russian hunting wagon.

Dormeuse. Old style of French travelling chariot which had arrangements for sleeping passengers on long journeys.

Dorsay. Name given to a coupé or Brougham suspended on both elliptic and C-springs and named after Count D'Orsay. A coupé-dorsay was a double suspension coupé.

Dos-à-Dos. A two wheeled cart (usually of the dog cart type) where four passengers sat back to back, two facing forward and two rearwards.

Dougherty Wagon. A particular style of travelling wagon used by the pioneers crossing the western plain of North America. Named after the builder.

Drag. A four-in-hand coach for private use.

Dray. A substantially built vehicle for moving heavy loads. In modern days used to describe a vehicle for carrying beer casks.

Dress Chariot. An impressive form of coach but smaller, seating only two people. Used for State ceremonies and occasions being of the best finish and appearance in the family colours.

Drosche/Droschke/Drosky. A particular type of four wheeled vehicle of Russia where the passengers sat astride a long bench.

Duc. A small French vehicle something like a Pony-Victoria.

Duquesita. A style of Victoria phaeton introduced by Hy Hooker & Co. of New Haven, Connecticut.

Eight Spring Caleche. Variety of caleche having eight springs in its suspension – four elliptics attached to the axles and four C-springs attached to the body by leather braces.

Elysian Chapel Cart. A style of two wheeled pleasure cart by James Henderson & Co. of Glasgow.

Epirhedum. A type of Roman vehicle.

Equirotal. Term applied to any vehicle having both front and rear wheels of the same diameter.

Essedum. Early style of English cart similar to the curricle.

Exercising Cart. Light type of road cart used merely for exercising horses.

Fiacre. French term for a public cab.

Float. Originally a large four wheeled vehicle with a flat body but later used to denote a two wheeled low tub shaped cart used by farmers and latterly by dairymen.

Fly. Old name for a two wheeled public cab. Also used to denote a fast moving coach similar to the stagecoach. Even used by some carriers to assume an air of speed to their delivery wagons.

Flying Coach. Early term for stagecoaches because of their speed compared to normal vehicles.

Four in Hand. Term used to describe a coach and four horses. Name of a coach driving club.

Fourgon. French term to denote a luggage vehicle which went ahead of the family carriage. In appearance a box body for the luggage with a cabriolet body for the servants.

Gadabout. American term for a small pleasure cart.

Gala Chariot. European state carriage with a vast amount of ornamentation for procession use.

German Wagon. Name given to a style of barouche in 1800 when first introduced into England from Germany. Also used in later years to describe a German type of freight wagon as built in Australasia.

Germantown. Style of Rockaway built in this town in Pennsylvania in 1826 by one C. J. Junkurth.

Gig. An eighteenth century two wheeled vehicle suspended on thoroughbraces. Later variations were the curricle, cabriolet, Dennett, Tilbury and Stanhope forms.

Gig variations

Dennett. A form of chaise using the three spring layout. Body was similar to that of the Tilbury or Stanhope gig.

Fantailed. A variation of the chaise popular in North America during the first quarter of the nineteenth century.

Gorst. A variation invented by Mr Gorst of Liverpool.

Howell. A design by Brewster, N.Y. of a gig body on a phaeton undergear for a Mr Howell.

Lawton. Named after the builder.

Liverpool. Named after the place of its origin.

Murrieta. Named after the designer.

Stanhope. Named after Fitzroy Stanhope to whose order it was built. A chaise suspended on four springs in an effort to provide a smoother ride.

Tilbury. Named after the coachbuilder.

Tub Bodied. The tub body as applied to the gig style of vehicle.

Go Cart. London name for a type of two wheeled cab with a deep cranked axle. Loosely applied to the wide range of cut down carriages used by the cab trade.

Governess Car. A light type of two wheeled wagonette or tub cart much used by governesses for the safe transit of children.

Grasshopper. A variety of chaise or whiskey of the end of the eighteenth century. Also called quakers-, serpentine- or sweeped-bottom chaises.

Growler. London term applied to a four wheeled Clarence cab.

Guagua. Early type of public omnibus used in Cuba.

Gurney. A style of cab patented by J. T. Gurney of Boston, Mass., U.S.A.

Gypsy Wagon. Name given to that type of living van used by gypsies and other travelling folk.

Hackerry. Passenger vehicle of India with canvas sides and top.

Hackney. Derived from a French word for a slow moving horse for hire. Became accepted term for a public vehicle for hire.

Hammock Carriage. A primitive form of carriage where the hammock was slung between posts attached to two axles.

Hansom. Name given to a style of safety cab invented by Joseph Hansom but much improved by John Chapman.

Harmamaxa. Ancient vehicle of Persia.

Hearse. An enclosed vehicle for carrying coffins. Usually four wheeled and sometimes very ornate but finished in sombre colours. Some varieties contrived to appear as normal coaches.

Hecca. A two wheeled cart with canvas top used in India.

Herdic. Type of Hackney cab invented by Peter Herdic of Williamsport, Pa., U.S.A.

Hook & Ladder Truck. Type of long four wheeled fire department vehicle which carried the long ladders and hooks used for fire-fighting.

Hoopoe. A form of Gypsy travelling wagon.

Hose Cart. A two wheeled cart carrying a large hosereel for the fire brigade.

Huckster Wagon. Name given to variety of wagon styles when owners attached their own fittings to render the vehicle more suitable for use for travelling salesmen.

Hurdle Cart. A style of dog cart.

Isia. A type of vehicle patented by Stanfield (1886) London.

Jaunting Car. A type of vehicle peculiar to Ireland in which the passengers are carried both sides facing outwards with their feet supported on boards on the outside of the wheels.

Jenny Lind. A style of buggy with rigid top and bracket front carried forward to form a dasher. Named after the famous singer.

Jersey Wagon. Early type of colonial wagon used by settlers in America in the mid eighteenth century. Large four wheeler with hoops and white canvas cover raised at the ends.

Jigger. A one horse streetcar of New York City.

Jogging Cart. A type of American village cart.

Juggernaut Car. A sacred vehicle of the Hindoo idol derived from a Hindoo word meaning 'Lord of the World' and under whose wheels people sacrificed themselves.

Jump Seat Wagon or Carriage. Any vehicle with folding or turn over seats to vary the carrying capacity.

Kibitka. A Russian cart with a tilt cover.

Kotcze. Hungarian term for coach.

Landau. A closed carriage of German origin having two folding heads and drop window glasses to render it usable as an open vehicle in fine weather. Various types evolved included stage, square, canoe, Sefton and Shelbourne.

Landaulette. Small version of its parent, the landau.

Leamington Cart. A variety of dog cart.

Limber. Fore part of a gun carriage consisting of pole, box body and carried on two wheels.

Lincika. A Russian carriage.

Lineika. A four passenger Russian Drosky.

Long Wagon. Early form of English travelling carriage of the fourteenth century.

Lorry/Lurry. Old English name for a freight vehicle with a flat body.

Lumber Wagon. A form of heavy wagon for freight hauling, sometimes applied to a timber wagon.

Magnetic Car. Ancient Chinese vehicle that had a magnetic figure with an outstretched hand which always pointed to the south.

Mail Coach. Introduced in 1784 for carrying Royal Mail between Bath and London. A heavy road coach carrying eight passengers and luggage with a special place for the mail under the feet of the armed guard at the rear.

Maltese Cart. Type of light two wheeled cart used by the military and drawn by one horse, pony or mule or in cases of emergency by two men. Presumably based on a design originating in Malta.

Malvern Phaeton. A type of park phaeton popular around 1850.

Milord. Name given to a popular cabriolet type carriage suspended on elliptic springs and being quite close to the ground, *c.* 1835.

Monalos. A variety of chaise with seat for one only.

Mountain Wagon. A substantial type of thoroughbrace travelling wagon popular in California and used for crossing mountain ranges.

Mud Wagon. American name for a light and cheaper type of road coach.

Oboze. A Russian freight wagon.

Omnibus. Derived from the Latin – for all. A closed vehicle of the wagonette family having side seats, panelled sides, rear entrance, many windows and fixed top. The term is generally attributed to George Shillibeer who introduced his particular type of vehicle to London from Paris.

Oxford Bounder/Oxford Dog Cart. Old variety of dog cart with large wheels and often driven in tandem.

Patrol Wagon. Chicago Police Department boasts of having introduced the first police patrol wagon in 1879.

Petorritum. A type of Roman vehicle.

Phaeton. Originally a high type of vehicle for driving by the owner. A four wheeled vehicle having no coachman's seat but often fitted with a hood. Name derived from Greek mythology. A selection of type names is given below but this is by no means exhaustive, there being many variations on the main style, many of these being named after their builder, designer, owner or a location which sounded appropriate at the time.

Phaeton variations

Alliance. A style of park phaeton popular during the

1850's.

Basket. A style of vehicle with basket work body.

Beaufort. Style built to the order of the Duke of Beaufort on a mail type of carriage.

Cab. Modified style of cabriolet phaeton being a marriage of the fore part of a perch high phaeton and the rear part of a two wheeled phaeton.

Cabriolet. The English four wheeled version of the French cabriolet.

Cob. Small size of Phaeton for a cob or small horse.

Crane Neck. Style having the perch swept up to allow the front wheels to lock under.

Demi-Mail. Lighter form of mail phaeton with elliptic springs and no perch.

Dog Cart. A style of four wheeled vehicle with dog cart body.

Drop Front. Design having a low, swept down front.

Equirotal. An unusual three wheeled phaeton invented by C. W. Saladee in 1856.

George IV. Old style with double perch and double suspension.

Mail. A design having a square box body with perch, raised driver's seat in front with hood over and seat for grooms at back. Suspended on two sets of telegraph springs.

Malvern. A type of park phaeton popular around 1850.

Park. Type of design for ladies to drive in the park.

Parisian. Term given to a particular form of light ladies' phaeton having graceful, angular lines of Parisian influence.

Perch-High. A high seat design on iron perches and four springs.

Pony. Small design to fit a pony.

Queen. A style of ladies' phaeton with a curved bottom.

Savanilla. Type used in Siam (Thailand).

Siamese. Style having two identical seats one behind the other.

Spider. A style with light frame and spindle seat instead of panels.

Stanhope. A style made at the instance of the Earl of Stanhope with square box body, four wheels suspended on platform springs with no perch. Front driving seat with no hood and a seat for grooms.

T-Cart. So named because having only one seat at the back it was T-shaped in plan.

Tub. So called because the body was tub shaped.

Victoria. Design having the characteristics of the Victoria.

Pilentum. Originally a Roman four wheeled carriage (covered). Early nineteenth century chariot in the style of a Droschke with a curved bottom line.

Pill Box. London term for a small compact little chariot used by doctors.

Plaustrum. A type of Roman vehicle.

Pole Cart. A style of road cart for two horses.

Polo Cart. A particular type of light road cart.

Post Chaise. Seventeenth century French vehicle which consisted of a chair suspended between two shafts and carried on two wheels. Later designs had a panelled body with front door again on two wheels. English variety was carried on four wheels and had a coupé body somewhat similar to a chariot. Driven postillion.

Post Omnibus. An omnibus for carrying mails in pre-railway days. Term reintroduced since the abandonment of railways in remote parts.

Prairie Schooner. Name given to the various travelling wagons used by the settlers, pioneers and immigrants on their various long journeys across prairies and ranges.

Quarterbus. Variety of four wheeled cab seating four and introduced into London in 1844 by a Mr Oley.

Racing Sulky. Name given to very light framing, wheels and seat used for racing.

Reckler. A cart used in India.

Rheda. A Roman type of vehicle.

Robinson Cab. Victoria Hansom.

Rockalet. A word coined to describe a small version of the rockaway.

Rockaway. Originated at Jamaica, Long Island, in 1830 and was an improvement on early wagons by virtue of being sprung. Later types were more like coaches although less sumptuous in their appointment. A four wheeled covered vehicle with curtained or panel sides with elliptic or platform springs.

Rolling Cart. Primitive type of English farm cart having thick elm wheels like rollers. Driver was called a 'high roller'.

Sarraaca. A Roman vehicle.

Scipea. A Roman vehicle.

Sedan Cab. Particular style of public cab which had the appearance of a sedan chair.

Sege. Old vehicle of the Azores with two wheels and drawn by two horses.

Shooting Brake. Variety of brake with facilities for carrying several passengers to a 'shoot' plus the sporting dogs.

Side Bar Wagon. A variety of wagon having side bar type suspension.

Sightseeing Wagon. American style of cross seat char-a-banc with the seats in tiers for easy viewing.

Skeleton Break. Basic skeleton framework of a four wheel vehicle with a high seat for the driver and a small platform for the groom. Used for 'breaking in' horses for vehicle use.

Skeleton Wagon. A four wheeled vehicle which had the bare framework and seat. Used for track work.

Sociable. A low hung four seat vehicle with doors and rear hood mounted on elliptic springs. Similar to the Shelbourne landau.

Sovereign. A more fancy design of the Clarence.

Sprinkler. Name for street watering cart.

Stage Coach. Originally similar to the mail coaches upon which they were modelled being large vehicles carrying a large number of passengers and their attendant luggage.

State Coach. An impressive style of coach with large glass windows and door sashes to enable the occupants to be better seen during state occasions.

Station Fly. A vehicle used for station work.

Stolk Jaerre/Stœlkjoerre. An early type of springless vehicle of Norway.

Suicide. Name given to gig with very high seat and a seat for the groom even higher behind. Used in Ireland.

Sulky. Name given to various styles of carriage suitable for the driver alone. Later types were light two wheeled vehicles used mainly on the track.

Sumpter Truck. Old name for a freight wagon.

Surrey. Four wheeled, four passenger vehicle similar to the spring wagon, phaeton or trap. With its pretty fringed top or later auto style top it was considered superior to the buggy.

Surrey Cart. A modern form of dog cart named after the county in England where built. Had stick seat and a rail round top of body. Whitechapel body.

Surrey Wagon. Modern form of road wagon but built upon the lines of the Surrey cart. Adaptation of dog cart to four wheeler, first produced by Jas B. Brewster & Co., New York, 1872.

Sytacle. An early form of vehicle.

T-Cart. A four wheeled, square bodied open phaeton with a single seat at the back, suspended on four elliptic springs.

Tally Ho. Popular American name for a four-in-hand coach.

Tandem Cart. Name given to a Dog Cart or similar which is driven with two horses, one before the other. 'Tandem' is the term used to denote two horses driven in this fashion.

Tandum. English variation of the French chaise, similar to the whiskey.

Tapcu. Name given to a type of French cart with hard riding qualities.

Tarantass. A type of Russian travelling carriage.

Tarenta. A Russian travelling carriage.

Tax Cart. English term applied originally to two wheel carts costing under £21 in 1843 because they were thus liable for a reduced scale of vehicle tax.

Telegraph. Name given to a style of the chaise with a body having space for dogs. Later used to describe early mail coaches and latterly to describe the system of springing on those coaches where four springs were connected to form a square.

Teleshka. A Russian vehicle.

Telyega/Telega. A Russian cart or wagon for carrying freight.

Thensa. A four wheeled Roman vehicle.

Tilbury. A two wheeled two seater invented by Tilbury the coachbuilder. Notable feature was its suspension which consisted of seven springs which together with other ironwork made it a heavy two wheeled cart.

Tilt Cart. Originally an old Scottish cart.

Tilt Van. Name given to a freight vehicle having a waterproof cover over hoops. Called fixed tilt or boarded tilt when cover was fastened to a close boarded roof, which extended part way down the sides.

To-Cart. French variation of the dog cart.

Tonga. A vehicle used in India.

Tram Car. Derived from its inventor Outram who invented the first tram road or Outramway.

Trap. A term used to cover many types of light two wheeled pleasure carts.

Tribus. A style of two wheeled cab invented by a Mr Harvey of London in 1844.

Triolet. An early French two wheeled vehicle suspended on just one half elliptic spring whose outer ends were connected to upright poles connected to the roof.

Troika. A type of Russian vehicle.

Trolley/Trolly/Trulley. Name given to a heavy freight vehicle; such as coal trolley, car trolley.

Truck. A two or four wheeled heavy vehicle for freight, usually with a flat body.

Tumbril. Originally a two wheeled military cart but later used to embrace dung carts and farm carts.

Turnout. A common term for any horse and vehicle combination as a whole.

Underdraw Wagon. A freight wagon which has the draught direct to the front axle.

Van. Originally a shortened version of the word caravan. Later used to embrace all kinds of commercial vehicles other than carts or wagons, but latterly closed types. Usually prefixed by other names such as laundry van or mail van.

Vehicle. Derived from the Latin *vehiculum* – a carriage; a general term for any kind of moving carriage.

Victoria. Various stories exist as to the naming of this particular design although the fact that it was named after the Queen is not denied. Basically a box driven carriage seating two facing forward with a hood. Swept down very low in the centre and having no doors.

Victoria Hansom. A type of Hansom cab with a moveable top invented in 1887 by J. C. Robinson, London.

Vis-à-Vis. From the French term meaning face-to-face. A small vehicle originally seating only two persons who sat facing each other fore-and-aft.

Voiture de Bains. A French vehicle for carrying bath tubs, or hot water for them.

Volante. A two wheeled vehicle used in Cuba with a body like a chaise.

Wagon/Waggon. From the German word *Wagen*. A word used to embrace all kinds of vehicles usually of the business variety and mostly four wheeled. N.B. In order to avoid confusion the spelling 'Wagon' has been used throughout the book although the *Oxford English Dictionary* defines both as permissible with 'waggon' as first choice. However American dictionaries list 'wagon' as the correct spelling and in the case of this book this version has been accepted to emphasize the international coverage of the text.

Wagonette/Wagonnette. Usually applied to a vehicle which had two longitudinal seats facing one another with the entrance at the back.

Wain. A farm wagon usually of the four wheeled type and sometimes fitted with end ladders for carrying light bulky loads.

Whiskey. An early form of chaise. A light vehicle on two wheels without a top. Derivation supposed to be because of its ability to move about smartly or whisk along.

Whitechapel Cart. A design of two wheeled dog cart derived from a butcher's cart and named after a part of London.

Whitechapel Wagon. American design of Whitechapel cart but carried on four wheels.

Windsor Wagon. A variety of square box buggy with side bars and cross springs.

Woosteree. Old New England term for a two wheel chaise with Tilbury body.

Wourst. A German type of hunting wagon loosely named after the famous sausage because of its long narrow shape making it easier to drive through the woods.

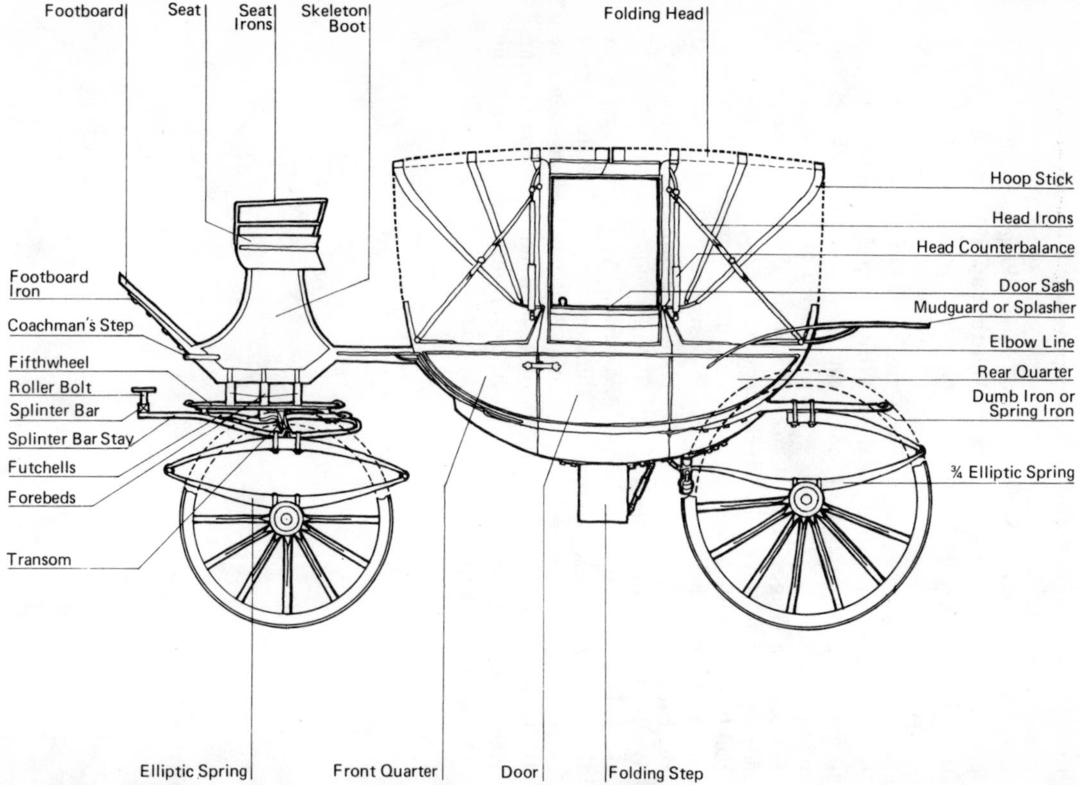

Footboard
Seat
Seat Irons
Skeleton Boot
Folding Head
Hoop Stick
Head Irons
Head Counterbalance
Door Sash
Mudguard or Splasher
Elbow Line
Rear Quarter
Dumb Iron or Spring Iron
¾ Elliptic Spring
Footboard Iron
Coachman's Step
Fifthwheel
Roller Bolt
Splinter Bar
Splinter Bar Stay
Futchells
Forebeds
Transom
Elliptic Spring
Front Quarter
Door
Folding Step

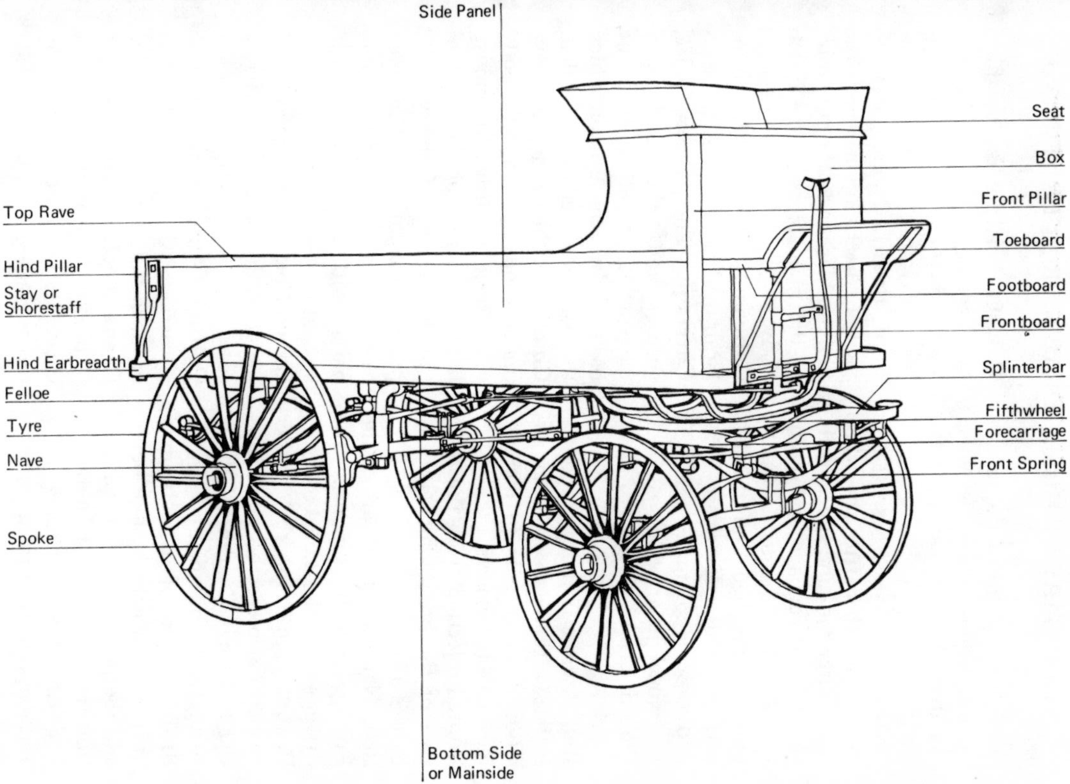
Side Panel
Seat
Box
Front Pillar
Toeboard
Footboard
Frontboard
Splinterbar
Fifthwheel
Forecarriage
Front Spring
Top Rave
Hind Pillar
Stay or Shorestaff
Hind Earbreadth
Felloe
Tyre
Nave
Spoke
Bottom Side or Mainside

GLOSSARY OF HORSE-DRAWN VEHICLE TERMS

Arm. Outer end of the axle or spindle which carries the wheel.

Ax Bed. Another name for axle bed.

Axle. Transverse shaft or spindle which carries the wheel at its outer ends and supports the rest of the carriage and body. Can be divided into the centre part or axle bed and the two extremities or axle arms.

Axlebox. Hard metal centre of the wheel nave which runs on the axle arm.

Bed. A cross framing timber.

Bolster. Transverse timber positioned above axle to increase clearance for wheels.

Boot. Projection from the main part of the body which usually carries a seat.

Box. Name for that part of the carriage which supports the driver's seat; also called a boot.

Brace. Name for the leather suspension pieces on perch carriages using C-springs, elbow springs or standards.

Bracket. Part of body framing at front to which the foot board and toe pieces are attached.

Budget. Box carried on travelling carriages containing tools and parts for repairs en route.

Calash. Small folding top for a carriage.

Cant. Term used to describe body curvature.

Cant Board. Name given to piece of board upon which the bodybuilder marks the curvature of the main parts of the coach body.

Capcase. Name given to circular or oval trunks.

Carriage. The wheels, axles, springs and other underbody parts which together form the basis of the vehicle upon which the body is placed or suspended.

Chamfer. The carving or shaving of wooden pieces of the body or carriage in order to remove harsh corners and so 'lighten' the appearance of the vehicle, provide decoration and in some cases reduce the weight of some parts without sacrificing the strength.

Coach Box. Open framework of metal supporting the driver's seat.

Collinge Axle. A patent type of carriage axle which had means of lubricating the wheels.

Crane Neck Perch. The style of perch which is swept up in a curve at the front to allow the forecarriage to lock under.

Dash or Dasher. The front panel of vehicle immediately behind the horse; originally made of iron framing covered with leather to protect occupants from mud thrown up by horses or from kicks.

Drag Staff. Short length of timber attached at one end to the vehicle axle and held up by a chain at the other; should the horse shie at a hill the drag staff is released to dig into the road and prevent the coach running backwards.

Earbreadth. Front and rear parts of the main bottom frame of the body; joined to the side raves or bottom sides.

Elbow Rail. Side piece of body framing roughly in the middle (or elbow height) to which lower and upper panels are attached.

Ex Bed. Another name for axle bed.

Felloes. The curved outside parts of a wheel on to which the tyre is put.

Fifth Wheel. Name given to the circle of iron which takes the wear and provides stability to the forecarriage as it is pivoted on the king pin or bolt.

Fore. Old name for front or forward.

Futchell or Fourchill. The longitudinal timbers of the fore-carriage to which is connected the splinter bar at the front and the swaybar at the rear.

Gear or Gearing. American term used to describe the under-gear or under carriage of a vehicle; the wheels, axles, springs and associated parts.

Glasses. Name for windows.

Hammercloth. Ornate cloth covering to the box supporting the coachman's seat.

Head. The top or hood of a carriage.

Hind. Old name for rear or back.

Hind Standard. An ornamental frame attached to the rear or hind beds of a coach.

Holders. Narrow strips of material secured to the rear of the coach body by staples and provided for the grooms to hold.

Hoop Tyre. Circular metal tyre shrunk on over the wheel rim to provide wearing surface.

Hounds. Longitudinal members of a farm wagon forecarriage.

Imperials. Large flat trunks fitted to the roof of coaches.

Jump Seat. A moveable seat.

King Bolt or Pin. Large metal pin or bolt which connects the forecarriage to the pillow of the body framing and around which the forecarriage pivots; also called perch bolt.

Knifeboard. Term used to describe the top deck of a public omnibus where the passengers sit back to back facing outwards.

Ladder. In addition to the usual meaning as regards gaining access to lofty places it is a term given to front and rear near horizontal extensions of farm carts so as to increase their capacity.

Leader. The first horse of a tandem; the first pair of horses in fours or sixes are called leaders.

Lining. Interior covering of a coach or carriage body.

Lining Out. Term used to describe the decoration of a vehicle by means of lines painted on, usually around the edges of panels or along spokes, wheel rims and other underbody parts.

Lock. Term used to describe the turning action of the forecarriage; variations such as 'quarter lock', 'full lock' denote the relevant degree of turning obtained.

Mail Axle. Improved type of axle first introduced for mail coaches, a type having provisions for lubrication of the hubs and better security of the wheels.

Mainside. Bottom side pieces of body framing.

Nave. The large centre part of the wheel.

Nunters. Small pieces of the frame which are attached to the hindbed.

Out to Out. System of measuring the track of a vehicle where the dimension is taken to the outsides of the two wheels on the same axle. Other systems were in-to-in or out-to-in, all giving slightly differing figures.

Patent Axle. Term loosely applied to the collinge axle which was originally patented but later produced by others.

Perch. Long piece of timber or iron which connects forecarriage and rear axle under the body.

Pillow. Transverse timber positioned between bolster and body to provide clearance for wheels.

Plate. Narrow strips of metal usually attached out of sight for the purpose of strengthening the body.

Platform Boot. Name given to an arrangement of ironwork and platform at the rear of the carriage whereon luggage may be carried.

Pole. Long straight timber connected to the front of the fore-carriage for means of steering the vehicle, and to which a pair of horses are attached, one on each side.

Postillion. Name given to the control of a pair or team of carriage horses by means of riding one of them.

Propstick. Short stick or pair which support the shafts of a two wheel cart in horizontal position.

Pump Handle. Projecting piece of iron which connects body to rear spring and supports a rumble seat.

Rave. A longitudinal framing timber of the body side sometimes called rails.

Roller Bolts. Upright projections on the splinter bar for attaching the traces for draught.

Roller Scotch. A small wooden roller hung near the rear wheel and dragged behind it when ascending a hill to prevent the wagon rolling back if the horses should fail.

Rumble. A seat at the rear of the vehicle behind the main part of the body.

Salisbury Boot. Originally name for the curved form of boot which supported the coachman's seat and which contained his budget. Later carriages had the boot framed into the body proper and the term became associated with a leather covered box placed under the driver's seat.

Sash. Frame enclosing the glass of a window or door.

Side Bar. A type of wooden spring. A long piece of wood attached to the lower outside edge of a wagon and connecting to the axles to form springing. Or may be attached to half elliptic springs which are in turn connected to the axles.

Skeleton Boot. A carriage boot supporting the coachman's seat made up of iron bars instead of being panelled; originally made detachable.

Skid Pan. Metal shoe positioned under rear wheel of vehicle when descending steep hills to increase friction; also known as a drug bat or a shoe.

Slider Bar. Rear transverse member of a farm wagon fore-carriage which slides beneath the coupling pole.

Speaking Tube. A metal and

rubber tube extending from the seat of a closed carriage to the driver for passing instructions to the coachman.

Splinter Bar. A bar attached to the front of the forecarriage for attaching the traces of a pair of horses.

Spring. Form of suspension to reduce the transmission of shocks to the body as the vehicle passes over uneven surfaces. Many shapes and varieties including elliptic, cee, grasshopper, whip, telegraph, mail, nutcracker, upright, elbow, side, torsion, etc.

Spring Shackle. Means of attaching end of spring to body or gearing.

Standard. An upright, pillar, or frame piece of a body.

Strakes. Curved metal pieces nailed to the outside rim of the wheel for wearing purposes before the advent of the hoop or single piece tyre.

Summers. Longitudinal bearers for the main bottom frame of vehicle body.

Swanneck Perch. Early form of perch which was curved upwards just behind the king bolt or wheel plate to allow the front wheels to lock round under the perch.

Swaybar. A wooden bar attached to the futchells and bearing under the bottom of the perch to steady the forecarriage turning on the king bolt.

Swordcase. A long narrow box attached to the back of the coach body and opening inside, originally used to contain swords.

Tailboard. The rear drop down portion of a cart or van body.

Tandem. Manner of driving where two horses are arranged one behind the other.

Thoroughbraces. Long multiple lengths of leather which formed the suspension for many of the old designs of coach.

Tiger. Name given to a groom of small stature who rode in the rumble or rear seat of an owner driven carriage.

Tilbury Spring or **Suspension.** An arrangement of springs for a two wheeled cart as devised by Tilbury the coachbuilder.

Tilt Cover. Flexible tarpaulin or canvas cover for a van.

Transom. The two main cross framing parts of the forecarriage between which is the fifthwheel.

Trimming. The interior furnishings of a carriage; seats, cushions, swabs, lining, hood and leather parts were fashioned by trimmers.

Trunk. Large fitted case or box

carried on a carriage usually at the rear.

Valance. The narrow strip of material round the inside of the fixed top on a vehicle.

Venetian. Row of angled wooden slats over an opening in the body so as to provide ventilation without observation or access to the interior.

Well. Sunken part of floor such as at rear of removal van.

Wells. Name given to fitted trunks hung under the carriage on either side of the perch.

Wheelers. The second horse in a tandem; in teams of four or more the pair nearest to the vehicle are wheelers.

Wheelplate. Plate of iron shaped as part of a circle under which the forecarriage turns and bears against. Later term is fifthwheel.

Whippletree. Horizontal wooden or metal bar attached to the trace chains of horses working in teams in order to divide the draught equally; also called whiffltree, evener, swing bar, single and double and triple trees.

Windlass.

i) a kind of ratchet tightening device placed at the end of leather braces so as to provide adjustment of the suspension.

ii) a drum or roller around which rope is passed, and by means of winding a vehicle can be loaded.